Leavenworth Papers

No. 12

Seek, Strike, and Destroy: U.S. Army Tank Destroyer Doctrine in World War II

by Dr. Christopher R. Gabel

Combat Studies Institute
U.S. Army Command and General Staff College
Fort Leavenworth, Kansas 66027-6900

September 1985

Library of Congress Cataloging-in-Publication Data

Gabel, Christopher R. (Christopher Richard), 1954-
  Seek, strike, and destroy.

  (Leavenworth papers; no. 12)
  "September 1985."
  Bibliography: p.
  1. World War, 1939-1945—Tank warfare. 2. Tank
destroyers—United States—History. I. Title.
II. Series.
D793.G33 1985   940.54'12'73   85-21296

Contents

Illustrations

Figures

Introduction

On 3 December 1941, the War Department inaugurated a military concept unique to the U.S. Army—the tank destroyer. The term "tank destroyer" (TD) evolved into a broad concept that included personnel, equipment, and units alike. Born of a desperate need to counter the mechanized might of the so-called blitzkrieg, tank destroyer doctrine involved the pooling of antitank weapons into battalions at the division echelon and higher and the massing of those battalions, when needed, into regimental-size groups or even brigades. Specially developed tank destroyer weapons incorporated great mobility and high firepower at the expense of armor protection. Tank destroyer personnel were imbued with an aggressive, elite spirit intended to counter the tank's psychological ascendancy on the battlefield. The tank destroyer motto—Seek, Strike, and Destroy—signified that tank destroyers were not to await enemy tank attacks passively in the manner of traditional antitank forces but were to seize the initiative and take the battle to the enemy. The tank destroyer shoulder patch, depicting a black panther crushing a tank in its jaws, symbolized the "TD" spirit.

The tank destroyer establishment came into being with the blessing of the Army Chief of Staff, George C. Marshall, and for a while seemed likely to take its place as a full-fledged arm of the service. However, on the battlefields of North Africa and western Europe, tank destroyers never lived up to expectations. Advocates of the tank destroyer concept have explained this failing by pointing out that the Germans rarely employed massed armor in the later stages of the war, thus precluding the need for a major antitank capability. In addition, most tank destoyer units employed expedient weapons that could not execute the principles of tank destroyer doctrine. Finally, apologists have noted that higher commanders tended to misuse the tank destroyers assigned to them by breaking up the TD battalions and utilizing the fragments in missions other than the aggressive, antiarmor role.

While each of these explanations for the failure of the tank destroyer concept has validity, none of them reaches the core of the problem: tank destroyer doctrine was fundamentally flawed. It is the purpose of this paper to show that the creators of the tank destroyer concept formulated their doctrine with an imperfect understanding of combined arms mechanized

1

2

warfare and thus created a doctrinal solution for a problem that did not exist as perceived. Not surprisingly, field commanders who received tank destroyer units refused to implement a doctrine that failed to account for the realities of the World War II battlefield. The inflexibility of tank destroyer doctrine resulted in its abandonment and led to the employment of tank destroyers in extradoctrinal roles, albeit with a surprising degree of success. The flaws inherent in tank destroyer doctrine, rather than the misuse of tank destroyers by higher commanders or deficiencies in equipment, prevented the tank destroyers from fulfilling their intended role. That the tank destroyers performed yeoman service in spite of doctrinal defects is to the credit of the American soldiers who, in essence, created a new doctrine in the field.

CHRISTOPHER R. GABEL
Combat Studies Institute
U.S. Army Command and General Staff College
Fort Leavenworth, Kansas

Antitank Evolution 1918—1941

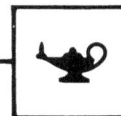

The advent of the armored fighting vehicle on the battlefields of World War I symbolized the beginning of a new age in ground warfare. The first tanks were clumsy, unreliable, difficult to operate, and capable of only limited participation in a combined arms team. Nonetheless, advocates of the tank believed that it possessed the capability to restore decisive maneuver to the trench-bound battlefield. First introduced by the British in the Battle of the Somme (1916), tanks eventually found their way into French and American armies as well.

The appearance of tanks in the Allied order of battle prompted the Germans to develop special means of countering them. German troops found that the lumbering British and French tanks were relatively immune to small-arms fire, but that no tank could survive a direct hit from artillery. Thus, the Germans employed 77-mm field guns in their forward defensive zones to serve in both antitank and close support roles. Some divisions maintained "flying squads" of 77-mm guns as a mobile antitank reserve. The Germans also developed a special armor-piercing rifle round and even designed a 13-mm antitank rifle.[1]

Inasmuch as the Germans manufactured only about twenty combat-worthy tanks during World War I and utilized another dozen captured French and British models, the Allies felt no need to develop a specialized antitank capability. A British pamphlet on antitank measures that the U.S. War Department reprinted and distributed makes this clear: "It is not considered either practicable or necessary, at any rate for the present, to introduce any special anti-tank gun; our existing artillery resources are regarded as being fully adequate to deal with tanks."[2] Although small-arms fire, aircraft, friendly tanks, and obstacles should all be considered as antitank resources, "experience shows that artillery fire forms the most effective defence against tanks, and that all other arms and weapons can only be regarded as subsidiary means."[3] The manual suggested that for antitank purposes artillery should be positioned in depth and should include mobile gun sections designated to reinforce threatened sectors at the first sign of an enemy tank attack,[4] much in the manner of the German "flying batteries."

3

Significantly, the pamphlet made clear that the tank's sole purpose was to support the infantry, which constituted the main threat in any attack:

> Tanks unaccompanied by infantry cannot achieve decisive success; they must be supported by infantry, who alone can clear and hold ground gained . . . . If the tanks succeed in penetrating the line, the [friendly] infantry must hold out and concentrate all their efforts on stopping the advance of the enemy's infantry, while the hostile tanks are dealt with by our artillery.
>
> The defeat of the enemy's infantry must therefore be the first consideration in all plans for anti-tank defence.[5]

This 1918 pamphlet expressed two concepts that would become part of U.S. Army doctrine for the next twenty years. The first concept concerned the role of the tank. The 1920 amendment to the National Defense Act abolished the autonomous Tank Corps and assigned all tanks to the Infantry. A 1922 field manual stated unequivocally that the tank existed solely "to facilitate the uninterrupted advance of the rifleman in the attack."[6] The second concept followed from the first: enemy attacks involving tanks could be countered by basically traditional means and did not necessitate a significantly specialized response.

Events in Europe during the interwar years did little to alert the U.S. Army to the growing threat posed by the tank. The largest European conflict of that period, the Spanish Civil War, witnessed the employment of tanks, but without decisive results. Some early antitank guns, in combination with traditional measures and expedients such as the Molotov cocktail (a hand-thrown incendiary device), seemed equal to the task of stopping the tank. Following that war, tank designers in Europe significantly upgraded tank capabilities, whereas antitank developers foundered in complacency.[7]

During the interwar period, great strides were also made in the evolution of tank doctrine. The British Army, prompted by such theorists as J. F. C. Fuller and B. H. Liddell Hart, was the first to experiment with large-scale mechanized forces, until budgetary and other constraints curtailed the continued development of armor doctrine. In Germany, the rearmament program instigated by Adolf Hitler in 1935 brought Heinz Guderian the opportunity to create the first panzer (tank) divisions, which would in time constitute the major challenge to American antitank capabilities. The panzer division was much more than just a force of massed tanks; it was a combined arms team centered around the tank. Each division included a panzer brigade, a motorized infantry brigade, a motorized artillery regiment, plus motorized reconnaissance, engineer, antitank, and antiaircraft battalions. Thus, the panzer division was capable of close integration among the arms, but at the *tank's* level of mobility, not that of the infantryman. Moreover, the panzer division could be broken down into combined arms battle groups, each one task-organized to fulfill a particular mission in combat. Guderian advocated the use of massed panzer divisions to strike at strategic objectives deep in the enemy rear.[8]

Compared to German interwar developments in armor, American progress in the field of antitank warfare lagged badly. Even so, the problem of

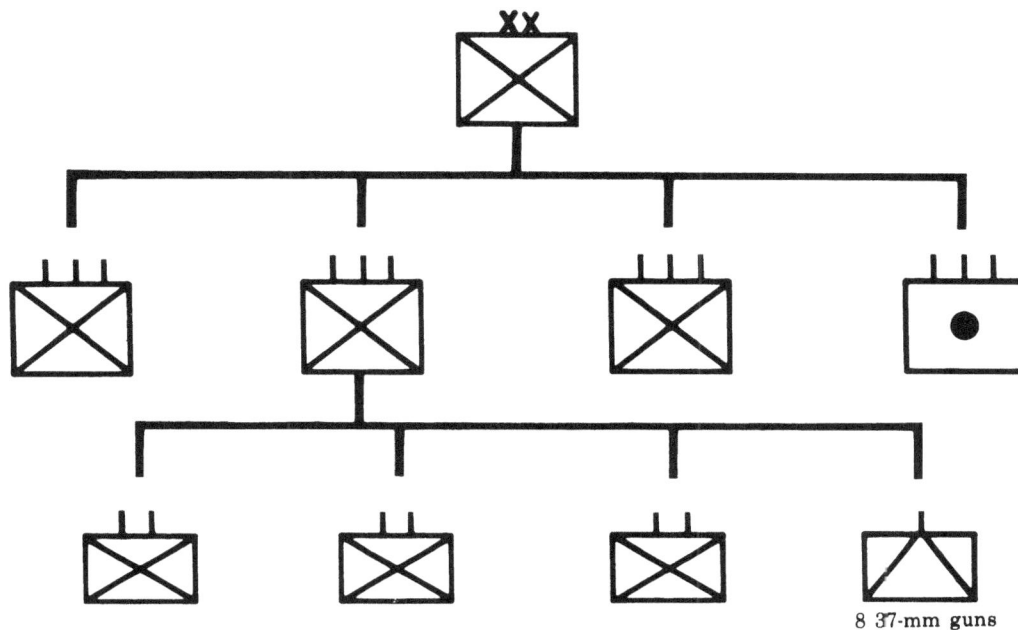

Figure 1. Proposed infantry division, 1938

stopping the tank was not completely ignored. The 1937 field tests undertaken by the 2d Division resulted a year later in recommendations that the Army adopt a triangular (three-regiment) infantry division as its basic fighting formation (see figure 1). The recommendations included placing an eight-gun antitank company in each regiment.[9] Although two years would pass before the War Department acted on those proposals, the 1937 tests had a profound effect upon Brigadier General Lesley J. McNair, 2d Division's chief of staff and director of the tests. McNair was destined to become intimately involved with both the organization of the U.S. Army for war and the development of its antitank policies.

In another positive development, the Command and General Staff School at Fort Leavenworth published, for instructional purposes, a comprehensive antitank manual. First appearing in 1936 as *Antitank Defense (Tentative)*, it was revised in 1939 and retitled *Antimechanized Defense (Tentative)*. *Antitank Defense* postulated the existence not only of regimental antitank companies similar to those proposed as a result of the 1937 division tests but also a divisional antitank battalion. The manual advocated an antitank defense-in-depth with the regimental antitank elements providing protection to the frontline troops and the antitank battalion guarding the division's flanks, protecting noninfantry elements, or reinforcing the regimental antitank forces, according to the situation. A fundamental premise of the manual was that the divisional antitank battalion must remain grouped and intact, to be massed where the tank threat was greatest. *Antitank Defense* proposed that antitank elements, especially the

divisional battalion, should be motorized and provided with reconnaissance assets so that a minimum of forces would be tied down to routine tasks, freeing the maximum possible forces to be held in readiness to meet the unexpected (see figure 2).[10] The antitank doctrine expressed in *Antitank Defense* was sound, clearly expressed, and feasible, if implemented with adequate weapons. Although not an official part of Armywide doctrine, *Antitank Defense* served as the basis for antitank instruction at the Army's highest tactical school. The commandant of the Command and General Staff School who authorized the 1939 revision entitled *Antimechanized Defense* was none other than General McNair.

The Army's official doctrine, as expressed in the 1939 *Field Service Regulations*, conformed in general to the precepts of *Antitank Defense*. Although the regulations perpetuated the World War I concept of utilizing artillery, aviation, friendly armored vehicles, and mines as antitank assets, it also specified that "the antitank cannon is of first importance in anti-mechanized defense. . . ."[11] It adopted the premise, found also in *Antitank Defense*, that local defense was the task of organic regimental antitank elements, and that the protection of the command as a whole was the responsibility of yet-to-be-created antitank units controlled by higher headquarters.[12]

Thus, by 1939, Army antitank doctrine included some sound fundamental principles, even though the Army had yet to establish the antitank units themselves. Nor did the Army possess a real antitank gun when *Antitank Defense* and the 1939 *Field Service Regulations* were written. In planning for fiscal year 1939, the general staff made a conscious decision to forego normal research and development procedures in order to procure some kind of existing antitank weapon immediately. As a consequence, the Ordnance Department found itself responsible for producing a copy of the German PAK 36, a 37-mm antitank weapon that was already nearing obsolescence. Production of the American version (which was undertaken without regard to patents or licensing laws) began in early 1940 and yielded some 2,500 weapons by the time the United States went to war.[13] Meanwhile, .50-caliber machine guns and antiquated field guns of 37-mm and 75-mm would also be pressed into antitank service.[14]

Germany's invasion of Poland on 1 September 1939 signaled the beginning of World War II and alerted the world to the potential of mechanized forces. Six panzer divisions spearheaded the pincers that enveloped and crushed the Polish Army in its frontier positions and brought the campaign to a close within a month. Western analysts were impressed by the so-called blitzkrieg, but most shared the attitude of the French high command that German successes of such magnitude were unlikely to be repeated against a first-rate opponent.

In the United States, the outbreak of war in Europe occasioned the beginnings of rearmament. General George C. Marshall, who became Army Chief of Staff on the same day that the war began, ordered the Army to adopt the triangular division that had been tested in 1937. As implemented in 1939, the triangular division's antitank assets were limited to twenty-four antitank guns under the control of division artillery.[15] This action raised the question of which arm was responsible for antitank combat, inas-

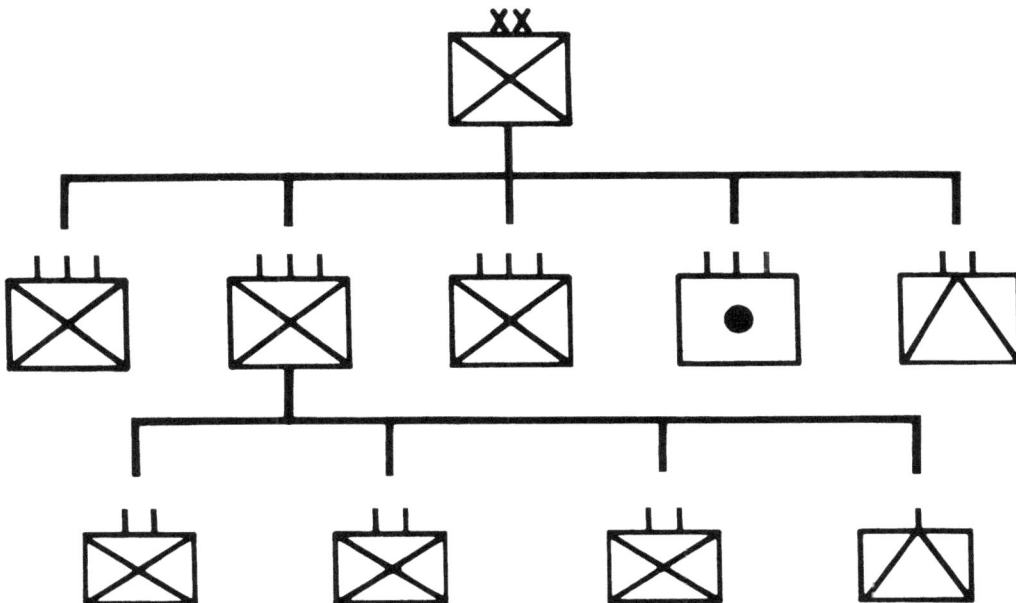

Figure 2. *Antitank Defense* proposal, 1936

much as the *Field Service Regulations* stated that antitank defense was primarily the concern of the Infantry.[16] The division of authority between Infantry and Field Artillery paralyzed the development of American antitank capabilities just when the need for haste was becoming manifest.

If any event could have galvanized the Army into seeing after its antitank capabilities, it should have been the stunning defeat of France in the spring of 1940. At this time, the German armed forces enjoyed no significant superiority in numbers of divisions over the western Allies (about 140 each) and were actually inferior in numbers of tanks (approximately 2,200 to 3,000).[17] However, the bulk of the Allied tanks were scattered by battalions along the front for World War I-style infantry support, whereas the German armor was gathered together into ten panzer divisions.

French antitank doctrine was unequal to the task of stopping massed panzers. The French clung to the World War I tenet that the tank existed to support the infantry and failed to consider the significance of a panzer division predicated upon massed tanks. Accordingly, French antitank doctrine called for the frontline infantry to allow the enemy tanks to pass by and then to rise up and engage the enemy infantry, which supposedly constituted the true threat. Meanwhile, the enemy tanks, meaningless without their infantry, would be destroyed by antitank guns organized in three echelons.[18]

The 37-mm antitank gun, the Army's first specialized antitank weapon

French faith in the antitank gun was absolute. To quote a French field manual, "At the present time, the antitank gun confronts the tank, as during the last war, the machine gun confronted the infantry."[19] Each French infantry division possessed fifty-eight antitank guns, yielding a ratio of ten antitank guns per kilometer of front. The French calculated that this concentration could cope with fifty enemy tanks per kilometer.[20]

Unfortunately, the main German panzer thrusts that crossed the frontier in 1940 struck at selected spots with concentrations of up to one hundred tanks per kilometer. Seven of the ten panzer divisions sprang through the Ardennes forest and shattered the weakest sector of the Allied front, along the Meuse River. Task-organized into battle groups, the massed panzer divisions punched through the linear French defenses and pressed on to reach the English Channel within two weeks of the start of the campaign. The pace of the panzer advance prevented the Allies from regaining their equilibrium or restoring a front line. Due largely to the efforts of the panzer divisions, the finest elements of the British and French Armies were either destroyed or pinned against the sea. Final defeat and capitulation of the French nation followed within a month.

The destruction of the French Army, widely regarded as the finest in western Europe if not the world, shocked Americans as the defeat of Poland had failed to do. Congress authorized the induction of the National Guard and Reserves in August and in September passed the nation's first peacetime selective service act. The Army implemented its Protective Mobilization Plan, which involved the activation of four full field armies headed by a general headquarters (GHQ). The GHQ chief of staff, who was responsible for organizing and training the ground forces, was Brigadier General McNair (McNair would become a lieutenant general within a year).

To Americans, it seemed clear that the principal agent of the Allies' demise had been the German panzers. The underestimation of armored warfare that had prevailed in the U.S. Army was displaced by an exaggerated fear of the tank that overlooked Allied strategic blunders in France and obscured the combined arms nature of the panzer division. A survivor of the French collapse reported simply that "the main cause of our failure to hold the Germans was the lack of efficient and sufficiently numerous antitank weapons. . . . Could the tanks have been stopped, the whole blitz would have crumbled."[21] Reports had it that 6,000 German tanks had simply inundated the French and British.[22] *Field Artillery Journal* maintained that some of these panzers were monsters of seventy tons,[23] more than three times the actual weight of the largest German tank in 1940.

American officers had cause for alarm, if not desperation, for as late as the summer of 1940, few of the artillerymen charged with antitank defense had ever seen a tank in action, let alone a mechanized formation, nor had they ever fired their inadequate weapons at a fast-moving target.[24] The assumption took hold that the infantry division was helpless in the face of a panzer attack, and some artillery officers discussed antitank combat in terms of last-ditch fighting by isolated antitank batteries.[25] The Field Artillery apparently assumed that its antitank guns were intended for the defense of the artillery and not of the division as a whole.

Although individual officers had become greatly concerned with the problem of stopping the tank, official reaction to the panzer triumph in

France was somewhat less than wholehearted. In the autumn of 1940, infantry regiments in a division were at last authorized an antitank company apiece.[26] These three companies, plus the existing antitank elements under division artillery, raised the triangular division's antitank complement from twenty-four to sixty-eight guns, only ten more than the number of pieces found in the discredited French division. The War Department issued a training memo on 23 September that recommended posting a minimum of antitank assets in the front line and holding the majority of guns in mobile reserve.[27] The new *Field Service Regulations* published in early 1941 reemphasized the importance of maintaining a defense-in-depth:

> Employment of antitank guns is based on a minimum of guns in position initially to cover obstacles and as a first echelon of defense, and a maximum of guns as a mobile reserve. Based on information of hostile mechanized forces, reserve guns are moved rapidly to previously reconnoitered locations and so disposed in depth as to permit timely and powerful reinforcement of areas threatened by hostile mechanized attack.[28]

In fact, *Field Service Regulations* of 1941 had little more to offer on antitank warfare than had the 1939 edition. The scheme proposed in *Antitank Defense*, with its divisional antitank battalion backing up the regimental antitank companies, remained superior to official doctrine.

In terms of actually creating competent and confident antitank units, little was accomplished in late 1940 and early 1941. The disorders resulting from the induction of civilian components hindered training of all sorts, as did the shortage of adequate equipment. Much antitank training took place with simulated weapons. The most serious problem was the continued division of branch authority over antitank matters. Neither Infantry nor Field Artillery embraced the antitank task as its own, meaning that there was no one agency to pursue doctrinal developments or provide training guidance to the field units. So far as the War Department knew, VI Corps was the only higher headquarters in the entire Army that issued any antitank training instructions.[29]

On 12 April 1941, General McNair was moved to remark: "It is beyond belief that so little could be done on the [antitank] question in view of all that has happened and is happening abroad. I for one have missed no opportunity to hammer for something real in the way of antitank defense, but so far have gotten nowhere. I have no reason now to feel encouraged but can only hope this apathy will not continue indefinitely."[30]

The Operations and Training Division (G3) of the War Department General Staff, headed by Brigadier General Harry L. Twaddle, made an attempt to break the logjam by hosting an antitank conference on 15 April. In attendance were representatives from Infantry, Field Artillery, Armored Force, Cavalry, Coast Artillery, GHQ, and War Plans Division. In general, the attendees concurred on the need to expedite the development of antitank capabilities and agreed that divisional antitank battalions would soon be authorized, but the conference failed to establish a consensus as to which

General of the Army George C. Marshall, who was deeply involved in pre-World War II force development

arm should be responsible for antitank developments. The Infantry representative stated that his arm should continue to administer to antitank defense because it possessed the "essential background and experience"—a curious argument when one considers the Infantry's unimpressive record of antitank development. Field Artillery claimed an interest on the grounds that it controlled the weapons most suitable to antitank combat. (In fact, antiaircraft guns, which came from Coast Artillery, not Field Artillery, would prove to be the best interim antitank weapons.) Cavalry also entered a bid for antitank responsibility, believing itself a branch that could "readily adapt itself to assuming what promise[d] to become a larger and larger task." (In other words, Cavalry was an arm in search of a mission, due to the refusal of its current chief to admit that the day of the horse had passed.) The Armored Force perceived antitank defense to be antithetical to its offensive philosophy and declined any interest in assuming responsibility. GHQ testified that the number of antitank guns in existing formations was adequate, but that their dispersal among several echelons rendered them ineffective. To remedy this situation, GHQ proposed that all antitank elements be removed from the line units and concentrated under a separate GHQ Antitank Force. In the end, G3 recommended to the Army Chief of Staff, General Marshall, that Infantry exercise jurisdiction over antitank matters until such a time as an official armored arm was established, whereupon Armor would assume responsibility, presumably whether Armor wanted to or not.[31]

General Andrew D. Bruce, head of the Planning Branch, a think tank for antitank warfare

At this juncture, General Marshall's patience ran out. A year earlier, he had reached the same impasse with regard to mechanized forces. His response in 1940 had been to withdraw all tanks from the existing arms and place them under the authority of a new "quasi-arm," the Armored Force. Marshall opted for a similar policy with antitank matters. On 14 May 1941, he instructed G3, War Department General Staff, to bypass the arms and assume the lead in antitank development:

> At the risk of placing G-3 in the operating field, I believe that for the solution of this problem you should take energetic and positive steps to push this matter as fast as humanly possible. The subject should be attacked with imagination and untiring effort. I believe that it is a function of the General Staff and should be carried through in your office. I do not want the question of another branch or arm brought up at this time.[32]

General Marshall went on to direct that G3 establish "a small planning and exploring branch" to study unsolved problems such as antitank warfare. G3 activated the Planning Branch on the following day, placing Lieutenant Colonel Andrew D. Bruce in charge.

Eleven days after its inception, Bruce's Planning Branch held a small antitank conference of its own. The conferees reaffirmed the need for a divisional antitank battalion (to be formed out of division artillery's antitank battery and platoons) to complement the regimental antitank companies. Accordingly, on 24 June 1941, the War Department ordered the prompt activation of an antitank battalion in each division, in time for participation in summer maneuvers.[33] Thus, the scheme first advanced in 1936 by *Antitank Defense* was at last realized: antitank companies in the regiments would be backed up by an antitank battalion under division control.

The antitank battalions activated by the divisions during the summer of 1941 varied considerably in composition. This was due, in part, to the fact that National Guard divisions remained in the four-regiment "square" configuration and did not adopt the "triangular" format until after Pearl Harbor (see figure 3). Typically, the battalions consisted of three to five batteries withdrawn from division artillery and were equipped with various mixes of 37-mm, 75-mm, and simulated guns.[34]

By 1941, however, *Antitank Defense* was no longer the latest word in countering armor. Major (later General) Albert C. Wedemeyer, a graduate of the German *Kriegsakademie*, proposed another train of development in an article published simultaneously by *Infantry Journal* and *Field Artillery Journal*. Given the tendency of German panzer divisions to mass rapidly against a selected point of the defender's line, Wedemeyer considered it vital that antitank forces also be capable of concentrating in critical areas of the front. "The bulk of antitank units [should] therefore [be] pooled in G.H.Q.," held in highly mobile, centrally located three-battalion groups, and attached to the field armies and corps threatened by tank attack. He proposed that the primary weapon of these formations should be mobile, heavily gunned "tank chasers." Wedemeyer suggested that medium tanks might fill that role.[35]

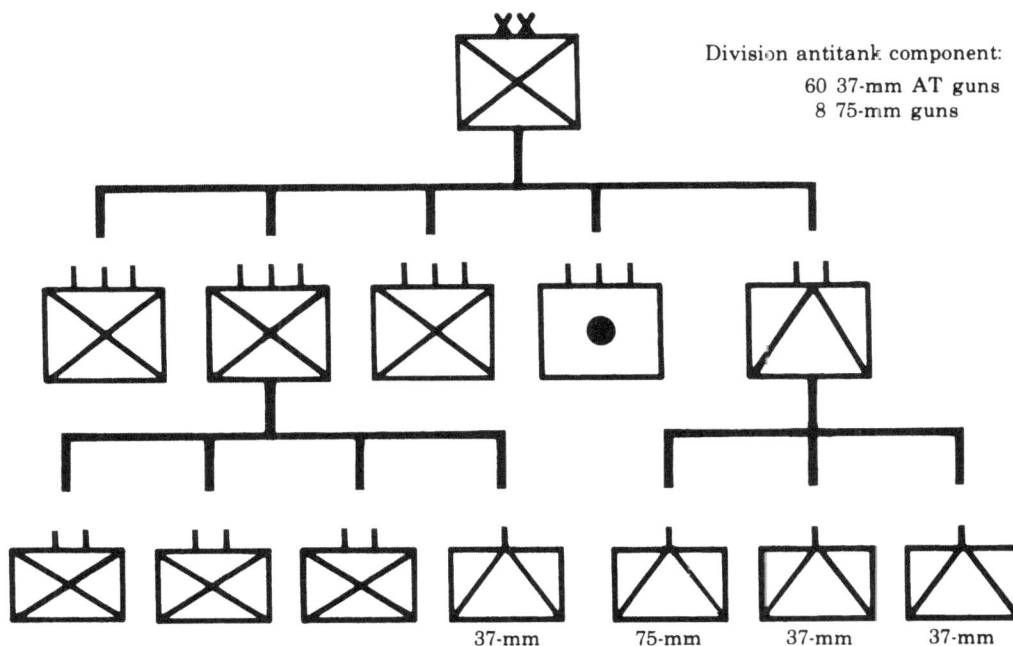

Division antitank component:
60 37-mm AT guns
8 75-mm guns

37-mm   75-mm   37-mm   37-mm

Figure 3. Triangular division, 1941 maneuvers

As early as 14 April 1941, General Marshall began thinking along similar lines. On that date, he issued a memo to G3, War Department General Staff, directing that "prompt consideration be given to the creation of highly mobile antitank-antiaircraft units as Corps and Army troops for use in meeting mechanized units. These units to be in addition to organic antitank weapons."[36] The representatives at the 15 April conference, as well as Bruce's Planning Branch, anticipated that such formations would indeed be established.[37]

The concept of gathering antitank assets to the upper echelons was very compatible with the policy of "streamlining and pooling" that underlay the U.S. Army's organization for World War II. Streamlining and pooling aimed at making the triangular division as lean as possible by removing any assets not needed for the division's basic mission and pooling those assets at higher echelons, from which they could be attached to the division according to prevailing combat conditions. This policy applied especially to antitank and antiaircraft formations that were inherently defensive in character.[38]

The concept of maintaining powerful upper-echelon antitank units can be viewed as a logical extrapolation of the *Antitank Defense* system. Just as *Antitank Defense's* divisional battalion supported the regimental antitank companies, so, too, would the corps, field army, and GHQ antitank units backstop the divisional antitank forces.

General McNair was a firm believer in streamlining and pooling, as well as in active antitank defense. On 8 August 1941, he directed Third Army to organize three provisional GHQ antitank groups (regiment-size formations) for participation in the autumn army-versus-army maneuvers (see figure 4). As raw material, Third Army utilized four 37-mm antitank battalions and five 75-mm battalions drawn from various artillery units. Each group consisted of three antitank battalions, a scout car platoon for reconnaissance, three engineer platoons, and three rifle platoons. The groups, which would be attached at the field army echelon, were trained to fulfill an "offensive role" that included vigorous reconnaissance, rapid movement to contact armored units before their tanks could deploy, and the destruction of enemy armor with massed gunfire.[39]

During September, Second Army faced Third Army in the largest field exercises in the nation's history. Second Army controlled I Armored Corps (two armored divisions) in the opening maneuver, and Third Army commanded the three GHQ antitank groups (in addition to the antitank forces in each division). At nearly every turn, the armored forces found themselves frustrated by antitank guns, a development that General McNair noted in his after-action critique: "An outstanding feature of the maneuver was the success attained in antitank defense, due primarily to guns. While terrain hampered armored operations, it seems clear that the mobile antitank gun defense now being developed gives promise of marked success."[40]

The results of tank-versus-antitank exercises were not as clear as General McNair implied. Significantly, only one battalion out of the three

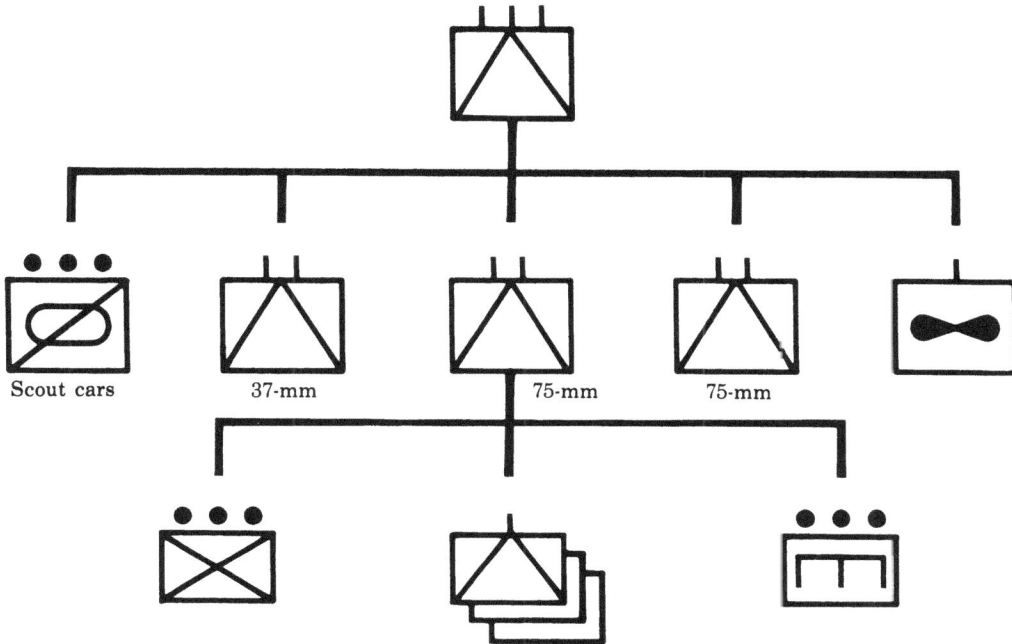

Figure 4. GHQ antitank group, 1941 maneuvers

antitank groups participated in a major antitank action during the two weeks of maneuvers. The vast majority of tanks "destroyed" fell to the antitank units organic to the divisions, not to the mobile groups. In addition, armored force personnel were quick to point out that the maneuvers' rule book was slanted in favor of the antitank, granting 37-mm guns and even .50-caliber machine guns an unwarranted degree of effectiveness against armor. The rules also stated that the only way a tank could "destroy" an antitank gun was by "overrunning" it, a dangerous proposition, indeed, given the exaggerated effectiveness of antitank weapons as prescribed by the rules. Observers noted that armor's doctrinal deficiencies, particularly its tendency to operate in all-tank formations, were as much as anything responsible for armor's frustration. They also reported that faith in the mobile antitank groups was lacking.[41] In sum, the Louisiana maneuvers demonstrated, if anything, the value of divisional antitank assets fighting in a relatively static mode and the need for the Armored Force to rethink its doctrine and force structure. In spite of General McNair's enthusiasm, the mobile antitank groups did not prove themselves in Louisiana.

The Carolinas maneuvers of November 1941 provided another tank-antitank test. Red Army (IV Corps) commanded I Armored Corps and its two armored divisions. Blue Army (First Army) received the three GHQ antitank groups and organized three more of its own: Tank Attacker-1 (TA-1), TA-2, and TA-3. TA-1, the most powerful of the three, included 93d Antitank Battalion, a provisional formation armed with experimental self-propelled guns (obsolete 75-mm field pieces mounted on half-tracks). Other elements of TA-1 included an infantry battalion, a field artillery regiment, a separate antitank company, a tank company, engineers, antiaircraft guns, and observation aviation, which made TA-1 a powerful, combined arms force in its own right (see figure 5). First Army directed that "the action of the detachment [TA-1] will always be offensive, moving to meet hostile threats and to destroy hostile forces before they can have decisive effect on the Army's operations."[42]

TA-1 had its moment of glory on 20 November when it received orders to destroy the Red 69th Armored Regiment which, in company with Head-quarters, 1st Armored Division, was stranded miles behind Blue lines near Albemarle, North Carolina. Supported by one of the GHQ antitank groups, TA-1 attacked the armored bivouac at 0615, just as the tanks were organizing a breakout attempt. Blue antitank guns quickly positioned themselves along every escape route and easily "destroyed" the Red tanks attempting to overrun them. Lacking infantry, the 69th could do little but charge the antitank guns with their tanks. The 93d Antitank Battalion drove its self-propelled weapons directly into the bivouac with guns blazing. The 69th disintegrated, forcing the division commander to flee in a liaison aircraft.[43]

Blue antitank forces as a whole performed better in the Carolinas maneuvers than they had in Louisiana. In one six-day exercise, the two Red armored divisions "lost" 844 tanks, 82 more than their combined tables of organization called for. (Tanks "destroyed" in the maneuvers each day returned to action at midnight.)

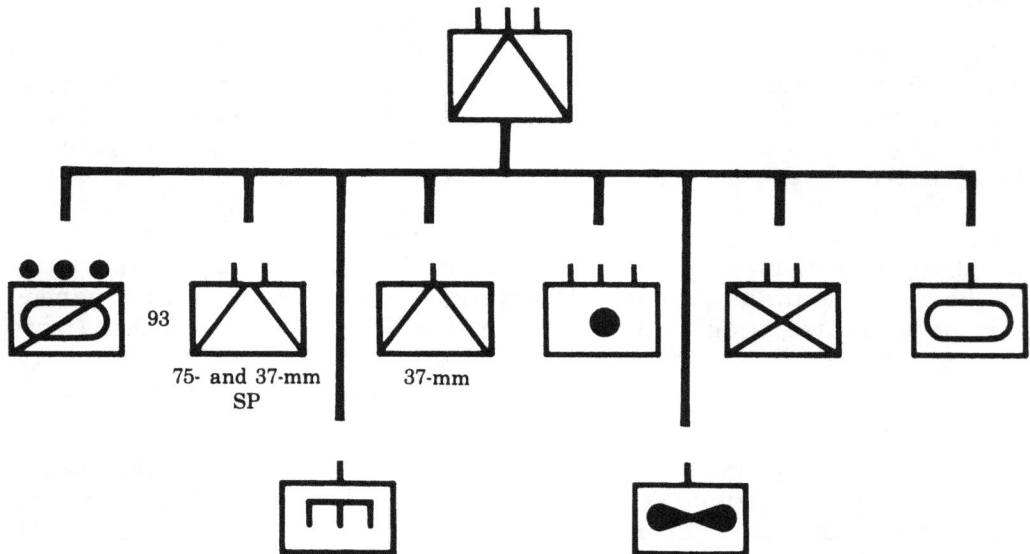

Figure 5. Tank Attacker Detachment No. 1, Carolinas maneuvers, 1941

Once more, however, a complete explanation of armor's problems in the Carolinas maneuvers involved far more than the antitank units it faced. As one observer noted, "It is believed success of AT units due to piecemeal [armored] attacks . . . rather than to AT units' effectiveness."[44] Of the experimental 93d Antitank Battalion, an observer report disclosed: "Its success in operations was the result of improper employment of armored units and the energy shown by its commander rather than from a proper conception of its employment on the part of higher unit commanders. . . ."[45] Observers noted repeatedly that the lack of sufficient infantry in armored units was a principal factor behind the high tank losses. The head of the Armored Force, Major General Jacob L. Devers, was even more succinct: "We were licked by a set of umpire rules."[46]

The Armored Force took its embarrassment to heart and, following the maneuvers, developed a new divisional organization that increased the proportion of infantry to tanks and significantly improved armor's capability to fight in balanced, combined arms teams. Antitank forces, having won an apparent victory in the maneuvers, would not undergo a similar critical reappraisal.

On 3 December 1941, Generals Marshall, McNair, and others met with the Secretary of War to discuss the lessons learned in the autumn maneuvers. McNair pointed out that the Armored Force, which had admittedly been mishandled on occasion, failed to achieve decisive results against the Army's new antitank forces. He recommended that the development of antitank forces be stressed.[47]

In fact, the War Department had already charted out an enormous antitank program. On 18 August, Lieutenant Colonel Bruce of the Planning Branch released an estimate, based on a fifty-five-division army, calling for 220 antitank battalions: 1 organic to each division, 55 pooled at corps and field army echelons, and 110 battalions as GHQ troops.[48] With four antitank battalions for each division, this program would have committed roughly one-fourth of the Army's ground fighting elements to the antitank role! A meeting in General Marshall's office on 7 October approved four battalions per division as a planning estimate and suggested the immediate activation of sixty-three battalions. Perhaps the most far-reaching result of this meeting was the decision to rename antitank battalions "tank destroyers," for psychological reasons.[49]

The date 27 November 1941 was a watershed in the history of the Army's antitank forces. A War Department letter of that date ordered the activation of fifty-three tank destroyer battalions under the direct control of GHQ, not of the line units. A further directive of 3 December removed all existing antitank battalions from their parent arms, redesignated them tank destroyer battalions, and placed them under GHQ as well.[50] Battalions withdrawn from infantry divisions received numbers in the 600s, those from armored divisions in the 700s, and those from field artillery units in the 800s. (The 93d Antitank Battalion of Albemarle fame, for example, became the 893d Tank Destroyer Battalion.)[51]

The letter of 27 November also ordered the activation of a Tank Destroyer Tactical and Firing Center under War Department supervision. Lieutenant Colonel Bruce, late of the Planning Branch, took command of the center when it commenced operations at Fort Meade, Maryland. The center's role was to serve as a developmental agency for doctrine and equipment and to provide centralized training for tank destroyer personnel and units.[52]

The significance of these developments was profound. By creating what amounted to a new arm of the service, the War Department surmounted the lethargy and apathy that had existed in the present arms and had stunted progress in the antitank field for so long. Also, by centralizing authority for antitank matters, the War Department assured the systematic development of tank destroyer doctrine, equipment, and training.

On the other hand, the directives of 27 November and 3 December eliminated the divisional antitank battalions by converting them into GHQ tank destroyer battalions. This left the division with the regimental antitank companies as its only organic antitank assets. The 1941 maneuvers had clearly and repeatedly proven the value of the divisional battalions, whereas the GHQ antitank forces had yet to conclusively demonstrate their worth against a doctrinally sound armored force. Moreover, the creation of a tank destroyer quasi-arm eliminated day-to-day contact between the Army's antitank forces and the other arms. The tank destroyers would develop their doctrine and train in relative isolation. Throughout its existence, the tank destroyer establishment would suffer from the amibiguity of its relationship to the rest of the Army.

The tank destroyer was born without an established doctrine or adequate equipment. Unknown to its creators, the tank destroyer force had less than a year to come of age before being thrust into combat.

The Synthesis of
Tank Destroyer Concepts

The year 1942 saw the tank destroyer program come to fruition. The accomplishments of that year included the finalization of official tank destroyer tables of organization, the formulation of a tank destroyer doctrine, the development of specialized tank destroyer equipment, and the establishment of training facilities and programs for tank destroyer personnel. By the end of the calendar year, tank destroyer forces were engaged in battle.

Two agencies were primarily responsible for the rapid development of the tank destroyer concept. One of these was Army Ground Forces (AGF), which on 9 March 1942 supplanted GHQ as the primary organization responsible for organizing and training ground combat elements. Lieutenant General McNair, by this time acknowledged as the father of the tank destroyers, commanded AGF. Thus, McNair bore the ultimate responsibility for tank destroyer organization, doctrine, and training.[1] The second agency involved was the Tank Destroyer Tactical and Firing Center under Colonel Bruce, which did the actual work of drawing up organizational charts, preparing field manuals, and training the tank destroyer troops.

One of the fundamental assumptions underlying the tank destroyer concept as it emerged in 1942 was the idea that stopping the tank had become a special problem that demanded a specialized response above and beyond general defensive measures. To General McNair, the solution to this problem was clear:

> The tank was introduced to protect against automatic small arms fire, which was developed so greatly during and since the [First] World War. Its answer is fire against which the tank does not protect—the antitank gun. That this answer failed [against the Germans in 1940] was due primarily to the pitifully inadequate number and power of French and British antitank guns, as well as their incorrect organization.[2]

McNair emphatically believed that the antidote to the tank was *not* one's own tanks: "Certainly it is poor economy to use a $35,000 medium tank to destroy another tank when the job can be done by a gun costing a fraction as much. Thus the friendly armored force is freed to attack a more proper target, the opposing force as a whole . . . ."[3]

Therefore, the task confronting Bruce and the Tank Destroyer Tactical and Firing Center was not simply one of finding a way to stop tanks, but rather one of developing a mode of antitank combat that freed other friendly forces for offensive operations. To meet this challenge, the tank destroyer creators adopted mass, mobility, firepower, and aggressiveness as the qualities that would enable tank destroyer elements to fulfill their mission.

The first concrete accomplishment of the Tank Destroyer Tactical and Firing Center was the issuance of tables of organization for the tank destroyer battalion, which became the basic tank destroyer unit. Fortunately, a prototypical tank destroyer battalion had been in existence since the summer of 1941, in the form of the 93d Antitank Battalion (redesignated the 893d Tank Destroyer in December). Experience in field trials and in the Carolinas maneuvers, where the 93d constituted part of TA-1, led to certain refinements, such as the elimination of light tanks from the reconnaissance company and the addition of infantry for security against hostile infiltrators.[4]

With this work in hand, the Tank Destroyer Tactical and Firing Center was able to issue three tentative tables of organization on 18 December 1941. Two of these formations were light battalions armed with 37-mm guns, which Bruce considered to be expedient organizations dictated by equipment availability.[5] The third type, designated the tank destroyer battalion, heavy (self-propelled [SP]), was Bruce's preferred formation and officially became the sole type of tank destroyer battalion on 5 June 1942 (see figure 6).[6]

The heavy, self-propelled tank destroyer battalion was a powerful formation comprising 35 officers and 807 enlisted men in its original configuration. (Incremental additions later raised the battalion establishment to an aggregate strength of 898.) It was led by a headquarters and headquarters company that consisted of a full staff plus communication, transportation, and motor maintenance platoons. The headquarters company was also the center for battalion supply. Serving as the battalion's eyes and ears was a reconnaissance company consisting of three reconnaissance platoons and a platoon of pioneers (a variety of combat engineers). The battalion's major fighting elements were its three tank destroyer companies, each of which commanded one platoon of light (37-mm) self-propelled guns and two of heavy (75-mm) self-propelled guns. Each platoon included two tank destroyer sections of two guns each, an antiaircraft section of two guns, and a twelve-man security section. All told, the heavy, self-propelled tank destroyer battalion fielded twenty-four 75-mm self-propelled antitank guns, twelve 37-mm self-propelled antitank guns, eighteen self-propelled antiaircraft guns, and 108 foot security troops.[7]

Inasmuch as antitank guns of the 37-mm type no longer appeared to be playing a significant role in the European war, the light platoon of the tank destroyer company was converted to a heavy platoon in a revised table of organization issued on 9 November 1942. The tank destroyer battalions that participated in the invasion of North Africa entered combat under the old organization.[8]

The Tank Destroyer Tactical and Firing Center also had antecedents to build upon when it turned to the codification of a tank destroyer doctrine in January 1942. During the 1930s, some officers, at least, had been instructed

35 officers
807 enlisted men
24 75-mm AT SP
12 37-mm AT SP**
18 37-mm AA SP

HQ

Light*
(37-mm)

Heavy
(75-mm)

Pioneer

HQ

2 guns each

2 guns

HQ

2 guns each

2 guns

Security
(12 EM)

Security
(12 EM)

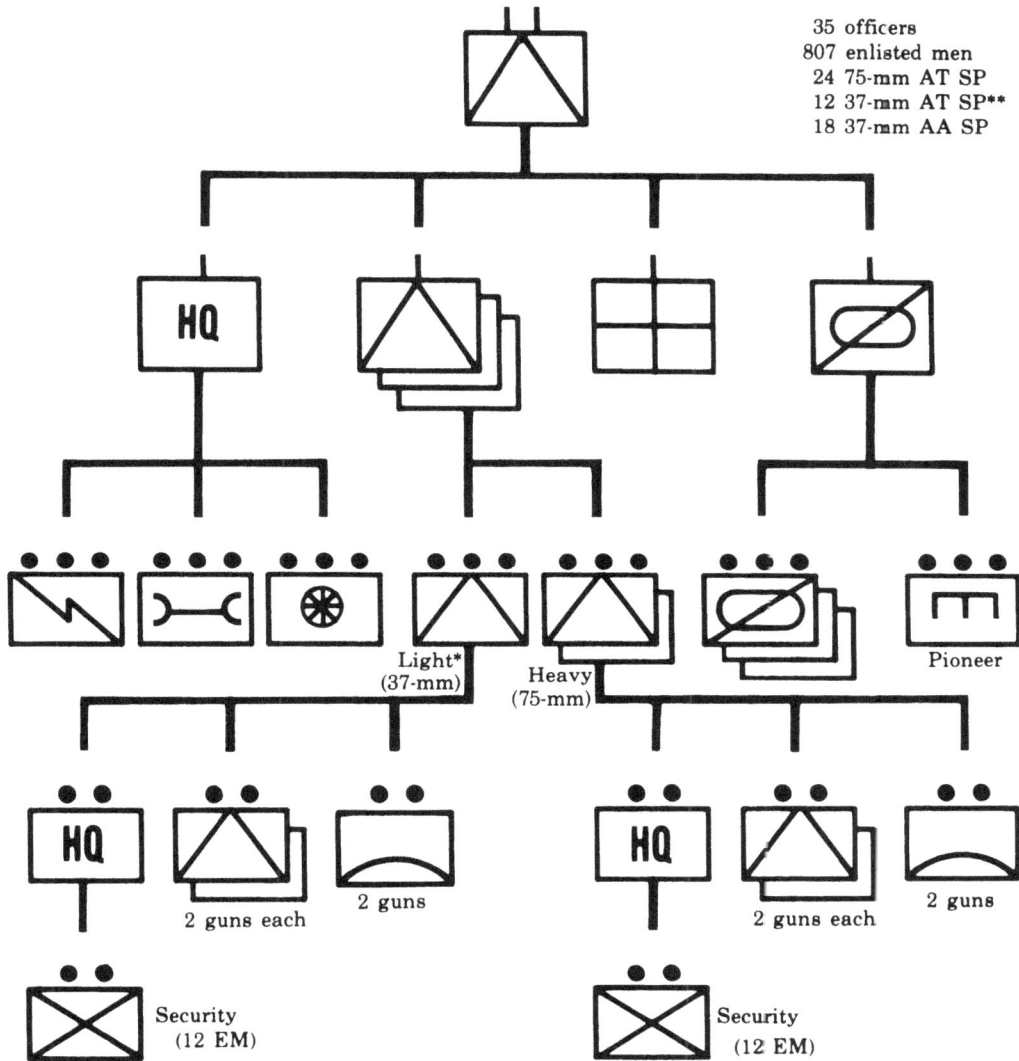

*Converted to heavy platoon, 9 November 1942
**Replaced by 75-mm weapons, 9 November 1942

Figure 6. Tank destroyer battalion, heavy (SP), 1942

in the tactics of the "antitank box," which was a static defense-in-depth consisting of antitank guns posted at the four corners of a rectangular "killing ground." The antitank box technique was not unlike some of the British and German antitank tactics practiced in the North African desert, but as conceived in the 1930s, it was too shallow and its guns (37-mm and .50-caliber) were inadequate for the 1940s.[9] In any event, the formulators of tank destroyer doctrine deliberately forswore any antitank concept that suggested a cordon defense. They delegated defense of the front lines to the regimental antitank assets organic to the division.

Instead of a cordon, tank destroyer doctrine embraced the principle of a massed antitank reserve that was propounded by *Antitank Defense,* first published at the Command and General Staff School in 1936. Tank destroyer battalions and even larger groupings would be held out of the line, ready to respond to tank threats at the front, flanks, or rear.

Following the defeat of Poland and France, these pre-blitzkrieg antitank concepts, fundamentally defensive in nature, suddenly appeared to be inadequate in the face of the panzer division's offensive might. It may be a personality trait of the American officer that, when confronted by an enemy possessing unprecedented offensive power, he will turn to offensive power as the countermeasure. However that may be, starting in early 1941, the idea of stopping tanks by means of offensive antitank measures began to take root in the U.S. Army.

The aggressive spirit inherent in the early tank destroyer concept is exemplified by the famous black panther emblem

An early manifestation of this trend came at the 15 April antitank conference hosted by G3, War Department General Staff. Although the branches could not arrive at a consensus regarding advocacy for antitank development, the conferees reportedly did concur on the need to develop an offensive antitank capability.[10] In the memo of 14 May with which he ordered the activation of Bruce's Planning Branch, General Marshall also called for an "offensive weapon and organization" to counter the tank.[11] General McNair concurred. In the closing remarks delivered at an antitank conference held in July 1941, he noted that in warfare, as in wrestling, "'There ain't no holt what can't be broke.'" But armored warfare was one such "holt"; breaking it required more than passive measures: "The counterattack long has been termed the soul of the defense. Defensive action against a tank attack calls for a counterattack in the same general manner as against the older forms of attack . . . . There is no reason why antitank guns, supported by infantry, cannot attack tanks just as infantry, supported by artillery, has attacked infantry in the past."[12]

The 1941 GHQ maneuvers reinforced the trend towards offensive antitank tactics. In ordering the creation of three antitank groups for the maneuvers, McNair directed that "the role of GHQ antitank groups is twofold: offensive and defensive, of which the former is the more important and hence the one to receive the greater emphasis in training."[13] First Army's specially developed antitank group, TA-1, was created with the understanding that "the action of the detachment will always be offensive . . . ."[14]

In retrospect, it would seem probable that the "destruction" of the 69th Armored Regiment at the hands of TA-1 during the Carolinas maneuvers became the model tank destroyer operation in the minds of the men who drew up tank destroyer doctrine. In that action, TA-1 located an all-tank force behind friendly lines, hunted it down, and "destroyed" it without interfering with friendly offensive operations elsewhere. The 93d Antitank Battalion, which with its self-propelled weapons was TA-1's most powerful element, formulated training notes and standing operating procedures based on its experiences in maneuvers and on lessons gleaned from exercises with a tank battalion.[15] Upon the activation of the Tank Destroyer Tactical and Firing Center in December 1941, the 93d, redesignated the 893d Tank Destroyer, became the center's first school troops. Its training notes went out to other battalions as guidance until official tank destroyer doctrine could be published. Its commander during the maneuvers, Colonel Richard G. Tindall, became the first commander of the center's unit training activity.[16]

In this manner, the idea of stopping tanks by means of offensive antitank measures, which originated among the Army's highest echelons, was apparently validated by some successful antitank actions in the maneuvers, even though many observers remained unconvinced. These doubters notwithstanding, the organization and offensive tactical procedures of the 93d Antitank Battalion became institutionalized throughout the tank destroyer establishment.

Unfortunately, this development sowed the seeds of future problems for the tank destroyers. For one, neither the German panzer divisions nor the U.S. Armored Force after 1942 conducted the sort of blindly aggressive all-tank operations that had set up the victory of TA-1 over the 69th Armored Regiment. Moreover, despite the official sanction given to offensive tank destroyer tactics, a significant body of opinion within the Army maintained, with justification, that antitank warfare was still intrinsically defensive in nature. Even General McNair wavered on this point. During the same speech in which he prescribed the counterattack as the centerpiece of antitank combat, McNair likened antitank forces to "seacoast defenses,"[17] a comparison that could scarcely be construed to suggest offensive qualities. Further, at the 7 October meeting in which the term "tank destroyer" was chosen for the new antitank service, McNair suggested that tank destroyer forces would "emplace and camouflage themselves" when faced by hostile tanks,[18] a practice that would seem to be out of character with the prevailing offensive mindedness.

The disparity between the defensive realities of antitank warfare and the offensive language was not resolved. The publication of an official tank destroyer doctrine perpetuated the ambiguity. Only after tank destroyer units had experienced combat would a serious reappraisal take place.

Tank destroyer doctrine attained official status in the form of the War Department's FM 18—5, *Tank Destroyer Field Manual, Organization and Tactics of Tank Destroyer Units*. Work on FM 18—5 began in January 1942 at the Tank Destroyer Tactical and Firing Center. A prepublication draft was distributed to tank destroyer units on 19 March. The official publication date was 16 June, only six months after the writing began.

FM 18—5 opened with a statement that established the specialist nature of the tank destroyer: "There is but one battle objective of tank destroyer units, this being plainly inferred by their designation. It is the destruction of hostile tanks. Throughout all phases of training and during preparation for combat, this objective will be kept in mind by all ranks."[19] The manual went on to describe the armored threat that the tank destroyers were created to meet. In many respects, that armored threat, as depicted in FM 18—5, was reminiscent of the U.S. Armored Force at the time of the 1941 maneuvers. For instance, the manual implied that light tanks constituted the major armored threat, just as light tanks predominated in the 1941 armored division. The manual portrayed tanks as operating in large masses that entered battle at top speed. It suggested that armored formations consisted of distinct tank, infantry, and artillery echelons, rather than the combined arms battle groups employed by the Germans (and adopted by the Armored Force in 1942). The tactics attributed to tanks included the overrunning of antitank guns, a practice thoroughly discredited in the 1941 maneuvers.[20]

FM 18—5 did not deny that armored forces were combined arms formations. It warned that infantry and artillery operating in conjunction with tanks would attempt to suppress antitank fire.[21] However, through means never fully spelled out, this cooperation among hostile arms would apparently be broken down, for FM 18—5 made it clear that tank destroyer units only engaged tanks.

FM 18—5 firmly embraced the concept of utilizing offensive operations to meet the tank threat:

> Tank destroyer units are employed offensively in large numbers, by rapid maneuver, and by surprise . . . . Offensive action allows the entire strength of a tank destroyer unit to be engaged against the enemy. For individual tank destroyers, offensive action consists of vigorous reconnaissance to locate hostile tanks and movement to advantageous positions from which to attack the enemy by fire. Tank destroyers avoid "slugging matches" with tanks, but compensate for their light armor and difficulty of concealment by exploitation of their mobility and superior observation.[22]

Tank destroyer forces would require special qualities: "The characteristics of tank destroyer units are mobility and a high degree of armor-piercing firepower, combined with light armor protection; strong defensive capacity against attacks of combat aviation; and flexibility of action permitted by generous endowment with means of communication."[23] These qualities had already been embodied in the battalion tables of organization and would also be reflected in the specifications developed for tank destroyer weapons.

Tank destroyer tactics as outlined in FM 18—5 built upon these same characteristics. Action would open with reconnaissance, which would begin early and be both continuous and extensive. The prescribed zone of responsibility for the tank destroyer battalion's reconnaissance company was a sector ten to twenty miles wide.[24] When enemy tank forces were located, the battalion's tank destroyer companies would hem in the enemy armor with surprise gunfire and maneuver against the flanks of the armored formation. In case of an encounter battle, the first tank destroyers to arrive on the scene were to engage the head of the enemy column, with subsequent tank destroyer elements maneuvering against flank and rear.[25]

FM 18—5 placed more emphasis on the ambush than on the encounter battle. Ambush positions were to be selected prior to contact with hostile armor. Tank destroyer elements would be positioned in depth, disposed in a checkerboard of mutually supporting firing positions.[26] Tank destroyers would not be tied to those positions but would be free to maneuver, for each tank destroyer weapon would ideally have a number of firing and cover positions. After firing three or four rounds from one position, the weapon would displace to another before retaliatory fire could be brought to bear against it. Maneuvering tank destroyers would be covered by those in firing positions.[27]

Obviously, FM 18—5 placed a high premium upon mobility and firepower for the successful execution of such operations:

> Rapidity of maneuver enables tank destroyer units to strike at vital objectives, fight on selected terrain, exercise pressure from varied and unexpected directions, and bring massed fire to bear in decisive areas. Tank destroyer units obtain results from rapidity and flexibility of action rather than by building up strongly organized positions. Tank destroyers depend for protection not on armor, but on speed and the use of cover and terrain. When maneuvering in the presence of the enemy they habitually move at the greatest speed permitted by the terrain.[28]

What would be the relationship between tank destroyers and other friendly combat forces? FM 18—5 specified that tank destroyer elements, like the battalions of *Antitank Defense*, constituted a mobile reserve, not a frontline defense.[29] Whether as a battalion attached to a division or a tank destroyer group pooled at the corps echelon or higher (usually three battalions plus elements of the other arms), the tank destroyers' job was to react en masse, in fire-department style, to enemy armored threats anywhere along the line.[30] The execution of such a mission required the existence of an armywide tank warning net and demanded road priority for tank destroyer units. FM 18—5 indicated that tank destroyers would actually engage enemy armor in the vicinity of friendly artillery.[31]

FM 18—5 affirmed that such operations would be "semi-independent" and asserted that tank destroyer battalions would of necessity be virtually self-contained units.[32] Such self-sufficiency, however, applied only in the face of enemy armor, for "tank destroyers are ill suited to close combat against strong forces of hostile foot troops."[33] When confronted by strong forces of enemy infantry and artillery, tank destroyer companies were actually to be kept to the rear, with only the reconnaissance company maintaining contact. In such situations, tank destroyers would become heavily dependent upon other friendly forces. Therefore, the manual urged that "calls for the assistance of other troops are made without hesitation when tank destroyers are confronted with situations with which they are not designed to cope."[34] Although FM 18—5 recommended that the "employment of tank destroyer units should be in close coordination with other troops,"[35] it did not spell out how that coordination was to be effected, nor did it clarify how such close coordination was to be reconciled with the tank destroyers' semi-independent mission.

In other words, FM 18—5 underestimated the significance of combined arms, not only as it applied to hostile armored forces, but also to the employment of the tank destroyers themselves. Interaction with the other arms took the form of "coordination," not integration of missions and means. Significantly, the only extensive reference to combined arms to be found in FM 18—5 was a two-page section found near the end of the manual under the chapter on training. It is clear that the formulators of tank destroyer doctrine believed that their special-purpose forces would be able to execute their semi-independent mission under narrowly defined and highly favorable circumstances: they would have thorough and timely intelligence; road priority; advantageous ground behind friendly lines; and an all-tank threat with friendly elements in close proximity, willing to adapt their actions in conformity with the tank destroyer battle.

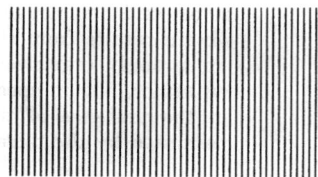

The 76-mm M-18 tank destroyer

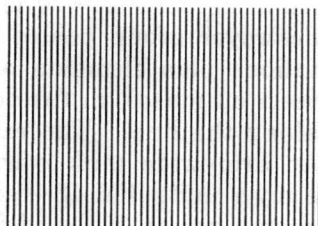

The execution of tank destroyer doctrine obviously placed a great deal of reliance on the ability of men and equipment to outmaneuver and outshoot enemy tanks. Early in 1942, when FM 18—5 was being written, most tank destroyer battalions possessed towed antitank guns drawn by standard trucks or half-tracks, even though the favored battalion table of organization called for self-propelled weapons. Bruce (who was promoted to brigadier general on 16 February) decided to adopt self-propelled weapons, even though General McNair continued to favor the towed gun. McNair insisted that the self-propelled gun was too large to be readily concealed, that it would be an unstable firing platform, and that it was less dependable and more expensive than the towed antitank gun.[36] Despite McNair's objections, General Marshall favored experiments with self-propelled mounts. McNair acceded, but he was never really reconciled to the self-propelled weapon.[37]

The specifications that Bruce laid down for the ideal tank destroyer weapon were very demanding: simple design, low cost, readily mass-produced, light weight, high mobility, with a three-inch gun to be manned by a crew of five.[38] The efforts of the Tank Destroyer Center to have such a design put into production met with resistance from the Ordnance Department, which pushed its own designs regardless of Bruce's requirements. A Special Armored Vehicle Board, chaired by Brigadier General W. B. Palmer, attempted to reconcile such disputes. Palmer noted that the representatives from the Tank Destroyer Center were inflexible in their demands, and that they were possibly asking too much in the requirements they put forth.[39]

Late in 1942, Bruce obtained approval from the Palmer Board for a tank destroyer design that met his specifications. The new weapon, designed from the ground up to be a tank destroyer, was orginally called the T-42. After a number of modifications, which included upgunning the original design significantly, the T-42 was eventually redesignated the T-70, and when accepted for full production, the Gun Motor Carriage M-18. The M-18 could achieve speeds of over fifty miles an hour and weighed less than twenty tons.[40] It had a ground pressure of only 11.9 pounds per square inch, less than twice that of a man (seven pounds per square inch), which ensured that the M-18 could traverse most of the ground that a foot soldier could.[41] Armed with a powerful 76-mm high-velocity gun, the M-18 was indeed an impressive weapon by 1942 standards. The one drawback to this, the "ideal" tank destroyer, was that it did not enter production until mid-1943.[42]

In the meantime, the tank destroyer battalions would have to make do with expedient weapons that could be quickly produced and, although far from ideal, would still allow training in tank destroyer doctrine. The first expedient, the M-3 Gun Motor Carriage, was a standard M-3 armored personnel carrier (the half-track) with a World War I-vintage 75-mm field piece mounted on the bed. Of eighty-six M-3s built in 1941, fifty went to the Philippines for use as self-propelled artillery; the remaining thirty-six were used to equip the 93d Antitank Battalion. The M-3 was standard equipment for tank destroyer battalions through 1942.[43] Another expedient, the M-6, was a light three-quarter-ton truck with a 37-mm gun mounted in the rear.

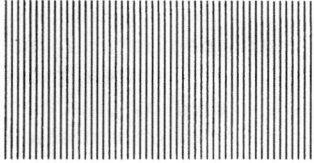

The M-3 tank destroyer

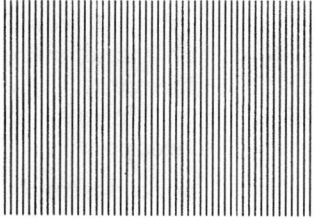

Except for a gun shield, the M-6 had no armor and was intended solely for training purposes. A third expedient, the M-10, is often considered to be the first true tank destroyer (in the sense of the term that denotes a weapons class). The M-10 utilized the chassis of the versatile M-4 medium tank (Sherman), was powered by reliable twin-diesel engines, and mounted an obsolete three-inch antiaircraft gun in a fully rotating open-topped turret.[44]

General Bruce disliked the expedient weapons, especially the M-10, which he believed was too heavy and slow to execute tank destroyer doctrine. He also feared that a large-scale M-10 production effort would delay the development of the M-18. AGF overruled Bruce's objections in May 1942, ensuring that in 1943 the M-10 would become the principal tank destroyer weapon.[45]

In the midst of writing doctrine and developing equipment specifications, the Tank Destroyer Tactical and Firing Center moved from its original home at Fort Meade, Maryland. Its destination was Killeen, Texas, where the War Department established Camp Hood on 30 January 1942, expressly for the use of the growing tank destroyer establishment.[46] There the center was redesignated the Tank Destroyer Command on 14 March 1942, but again

The M-6 tank destroyer

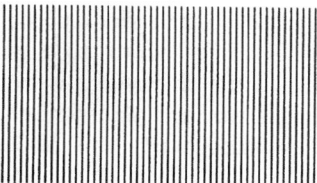

renamed the Tank Destroyer Center on 17 August. Camp Hood became the nexus of all tank destroyer activity, from the training of individuals to the activation of units and the development of doctrine and equipment.[47]

The heart of the Camp Hood establishment was the Unit Training Center, which organized and trained new battalions. It was eventually augmented by an Individual Training Center and a Replacement Training Center that accommodated personnel not yet assigned to battalions. A Tank Destroyer School provided specialized technical training to key officers and men. Eventually Camp Hood also came to include a Tank Destroyer Officer Candidate School. Camp Hood was also home to the Tank Destroyer Board, which wrote doctrine and studied technical matters involving equipment and weapons.

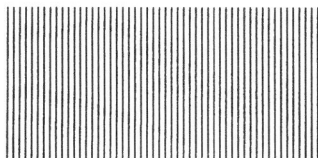

The M-10 tank destroyer

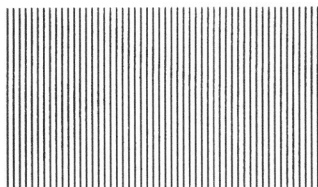

Training at Camp Hood was in large measure driven by the extraordinary emphasis that FM 18—5 placed on the élan and spirit of tank destroyer personnel. The manual called for "the inculcation of courageous but intelligent aggressiveness, the willingness to assume responsibility in the absence of orders, and the exercise of initiative and forethought in making instantaneous decisions to meet any change in any situation."[48] Thus, a "major objective of training must be the development of aggressive individuals and units whose skill with weapons have instilled in them confidence in their ability to destroy the enemy both at long range and in close combat."[49]

The "close combat" referred to was also discussed in FM 18—5 under the heading, "Dismounted Tank Hunting." Tank hunting, which was to be conducted by crews from disabled tank destroyers and by the battalion security elements, involved both ambushing tanks on the move and raiding tank parks with small arms, grenades, mines, and improvised weapons.[50]

An important feature of the Camp Hood training facilities was the Tank Hunting Course (later renamed Battle Conditioning), an innovative course designed to acquaint personnel with dismounted combat. Patterned after courses used in the training of British commandos, the Tank Hunting Course in many ways epitomized the essence of tank destroyer training. It consisted of a simulated battlefield that the trainees negotiated while, for the first time in Army history, live fire grazed overhead. The course included a simulated "Nazi village" complete with surprise targets and traps.

As the course evolved in sophistication, trainees eventually spent a full week on it under battle conditions.[51] Excellent gunnery ranges and vast areas of open ground facilitated the training of tank destroyer personnel and units in the more conventional antitank skills.

By World War II standards, the training program at Camp Hood ranked with the best. The camp grew into an enormous complex that at its peak had twenty-eight battalions and eight groups in training at one time. Although other branches of the Army were using some of the facilities by the end of the war, Camp Hood remained the focal point of tank destroyer development and training.

The M-4 Sherman tank, which provided the chassis for the M-10 tank destroyer

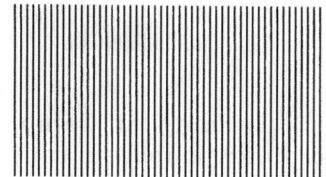

However, even as the first tank destroyer units underwent preparations for their first trial by combat, some serious problems within the tank destroyer establishment were becoming manifest. One of these was the relatively unproven status of tank destroyer doctrine. FM 18—5 had been hurriedly produced at Camp Hood in relative isolation from the rest of the Army. Neither the full doctrine nor the newer self-propelled weapons had ever undergone large-scale maneuvers in conjunction with the other arms.

Furthermore, General Bruce himself was dissatisfied with at least one major aspect of tank destroyer doctrine. On 7 January 1942 and again on 2 June, he unsuccessfully recommended to McNair that a tank destroyer battalion be made an organic element of each division and that all battalions in a reserve status be assigned specifically to some command.[52] Bruce feared that under the loose attachment and pooling policies favored by General McNair that tank destroyer units would be preyed upon for replacements for the line units. On the other hand, if tank destroyers were an integral part of the division or corps, Bruce felt that it would be in the better interests of the higher commanders to protect the integrity of tank destroyer units.[53]

Another problem that marred the tank destroyer program in its infancy was the abbreviated training time that some of the early battalions received. AGF timetables dictated that several battalions undergo as little as seven weeks of training before being shipped out for North Africa, rather than the two to three months normally alloted to unit training. Consequently, even some of the best trained of the tank destroyer personnel had reservations about their qualifications for combat. In addition, the deliberate cultivation of elan was not equally successful in all individuals, and some trainees questioned the value of such melodramatic and dangerous aspects of tank destroyer doctrine as dismounted tank hunting.[54]

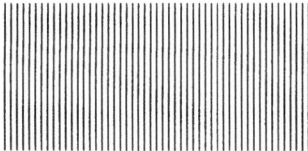

The M-3 tank destroyer during training

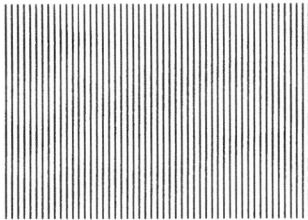

Much of the weaponry that the tank destroyer units employed in their combat initiation was expedient equipment that would make the execution of doctrine even harder. The M-6 was virtually unarmored, badly undergunned, and was never intended for combat, but it saw action in North Africa. The M-3 was little better, especially considering that the poorly armored and armed half-track would be engaging some of the world's best tanks.[55] General Bruce disliked the M-10, even though it was by far the best of the expedient weapons.

The most serious problem facing the tank destroyers in 1942 was the unpleasant fact that they were joining an Army that was largely ignorant of tank destroyer doctrine. A radio warning net, road priority, and coordination with other arms were vital to the tank destroyer mission, but all of these factors depended upon higher commanders who were poorly informed, if not wholly misinformed, about tank destroyers. To correct this situation,

General Bruce held the first of a series of indoctrination courses for generals and general staff officers on 30 November 1942—three weeks after Operation Torch began and eight days after the first tank destroyer battalion entered combat in North Africa.[56]

Tank Destroyers Under Fire

The war that awaited the U.S. Army in North Africa did not lend itself to the successful implementation of tank destroyer doctrine. The tank destroyer concept arose from a perceived need to counter the blitzkrieg, but in North Africa, the Allies, not the Axis, held the initiative. Moreover, tank destroyers discovered that German panzer doctrine bore little relationship to the headstrong tank tactics described in FM 18—5.

The most outstanding characteristic of German armored doctrine was the close integration of tanks, antitank guns, infantry, artillery, and aircraft into a combined arms team. As the British Eighth Army had already learned at great cost, German tanks almost invariably operated under the protective fire of a superb antitank screen. Typically, fearsome 88-mm antiaircraft-antitank guns, flanked by lighter pieces and protected by infantry, covered all German tank movements from concealed overwatch positions. Even when on the offensive, the Germans made every effort to support tank elements with antitank and artillery pieces. The British veterans knew well what the Americans were to learn: any attempt by tanks (or tank destroyers) to attack German mechanized elements, even those that appeared to be isolated and vulnerable, was likely to bring down a murderous converging fire from concealed antitank guns. Any Allied attack that did not provide for the neutralization of this antitank defense risked defeat and disaster.[1]

The tank destroyers would even find it difficult to stand on the defensive and ambush attacking German armor, for German tanks rarely attacked blindly or recklessly. An American armored officer reported that "when the German tanks come out, they stay out of range and sit and watch. Then they move a little, stop, and watch some more. They have excellent glasses [binoculars] and they use them carefully. They always seem to make sure of what they are going to do and where they are going before they move . . . ."[2] Major General Orlando Ward, commander of the 1st Armored Division in Tunisia, remarked that advancing German tanks sometimes moved so slowly that it was necessary for the observer to line up the German vehicles against a terrain feature in order to be sure that they were moving at all.[3]

33

34

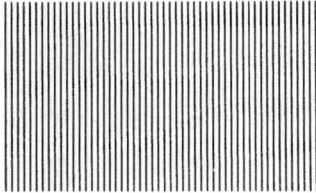

The German dual-purpose 88-mm antiaircraft-antitank gun

Typically, German tanks in the attack enjoyed the close cooperation of the other arms. Not only did the advancing panzers endeavor to bring their antitank screen and supporting artillery with them, but infantry would also be available to reconnoiter minefields and assist the tanks in utilizing every available terrain feature. The actual tank assault involved the support of artillery, infantry, and aircraft that helped neutralize the defender's antitank guns and create gaps in his defenses.[4]

Thus, the tank destroyers would find themselves at an immediate disadvantage. Their doctrine, force structuring, and weaponry prepared them to deal exclusively with tanks. In North Africa, the battle was not tank destroyer against tank but tank destroyer against an integrated, combined arms force conducting a skillful defense.

The qualitative superiority of German weaponry made it even harder for tank destroyers to execute their mission. FM 18—5 implied that tank destroyers would enjoy a significant superiority in firepower over enemy armor. By 1943, however, the German arsenal included the Mark IV panzer, mounting a long-barreled, high-velocity 75-mm gun that fired a tungsten carbide antitank round, and the massive Mark VI Tiger tank, which carried a version of the deadly 88-mm gun. By comparison, the expedient M-3 tank destroyer mounted a 75-mm gun (originally designed in 1897) that was not really an antitank gun at all. With a maximum armor thickness of .625 inches, the M-3 was terribly vulnerable to all but small-arms fire.[5] The M-6 was much worse. In the words of an AGF observer, "The sending of such a patently inadequate destroyer into combat can at best be termed a tragic mistake."[6] Its only armor was a .25-inch gun shield. The gun itself was the 37-mm antitank piece that FM 18—5 said was effective to a range of five hundred yards.[7] In practice, the 37-mm was effective only against the sides and rears of most tanks, and that at under four hundred yards.[8] One 37-mm gun of the 601st Tank Destroyer Battalion scored five hits on a German Mark IV at one thousand yards with no observed effect.[9] Against the Tiger, 37-mm guns were ineffective at virtually any range.

A captured Mark IV panzer mounting the high-velocity 75-mm gun

Significantly, the organic antitank gun of the U.S. infantry division was the same inadequate 37-mm weapon. Tank destroyer doctrine assumed that the infantry would be capable of basic self-defense against tanks so that tank destroyers could be kept back in reserve. In 1942 and 1943, organic antitank defense in the infantry division consisted of an antitank company in each regiment, plus a platoon in each rifle battalion, all armed with the 37-mm gun. Infantry antitank gunners reported that the towed 37-mm was truly effective against tanks only if perfectly camouflaged and fired at point-blank range.[10] A hollow-charge, rocket-propelled antitank grenade (the bazooka) became available in the middle of the Tunisian campaign, but this, too, was a short-range weapon, and the infantry had no training in its use. Tanks and tank destroyers would be pressed into frontline defense to help protect the infantry from tanks, in direct contradiction to the doctrine of both arms.

American forces attained a semblance of qualitative parity with the Germans in antitank firepower late in the Tunisian campaign with the advent of the M-10 tank destroyer. This weapon, with its three-inch, high-velocity gun, fully rotating turret, and robust tank chassis was indeed an excellent weapon by 1943 standards.[11] The similarly armed M-18, which first saw combat in Italy, was also a welcome addition to the arsenal. Events would prove, however, that even when armed with adequate weapons, the tank destroyers could do little to alter the tactical and strategic circumstances that militated against their employment in accordance with doctrine. The division commanders at the front could hardly be expected to allow the thirty-six self-propelled guns of each tank destroyer battalion to lay idle simply because battlefield realities did not conform with FM 18—5. Thus, the stage was set for wide-scale misemployment of tank destroyers.

A total of seven tank destroyer battalions participated in the North African campaign, which began on 8 November 1942 with Allied landings in Morocco and Algeria and ended in May 1943 with the capture of Tunis and Bizerte in Tunisia. Two battalions, the 601st and 701st, were the only ones to see action until mid-February. These units were originally drawn from the 1st Infantry and 1st Armored Divisions, respectively. They were organized under the 8 June 1942 tables (one of the three platoons in each company being a light platoon) and were equipped with the M-3 and M-6 weapons.

The honor of being the first tank destroyer battalion to see combat fell to the 701st. On 22 November 1942, Company B of the 701st, with a reconnaissance platoon attached, arrived in Feriana, Tunisia, after a six-day road march. At Feriana, the company commander received orders to assault and capture the town of Gafsa, a mission completely at variance with tank destroyer doctrine. Company B approached the task without infantry or artillery support and in the "absolute absence of any information on the enemy forces."[12] Upon reaching Gafsa, the company's two M-3 platoons deployed and shot their way into the town. (The company commander wisely kept his platoon of M-6s in reserve.) Surprisingly, the attack succeeded without loss. The M-3s pushed on and managed to ambush a body of enemy tanks at nearby El Guettar, destroying four without losing an M-3. On the next day, Company B drove the enemy out of Sbeitla in a similar operation, destroying eleven Axis tanks in the process. The company commander attributed this feat to "our boldness [that] was matched only by the enemy's utter disregard for the remotest pretense of local security."[13]

In these first three tank destroyer actions, Company B took 400 prisoners and claimed fifteen enemy tanks destroyed.[14] Back at Camp Hood, instructors at the tank destroyer school passed this account on to their students but accompanied it with a warning: "Do not expect to use your tank destroyers in this manner and succeed in a majority of cases."[15]

The curious engagements at Gafsa and Sbeitla were an encouraging initiation to combat, but they did little to test the capabilities of tank destroyers in their primary mission. Such an opportunity arose between 14 and 22 February 1943 in the course of a German counteroffensive known generally as the battle of Kasserine Pass. Along with other elements in the U.S. Army, the tank destroyers were found wanting.

Like most U.S. units in Tunisia, the tank destroyer battalions involved in the Kasserine battle were fragmented and dispersed. The 601st and 701st Tank Destoyer Battalions, still scattered about in companies and by now understrength due to attrition, were thrashed piecemeal by Field Marshal Erwin Rommel's veterans of the Libyan desert. The initial 14 February assault of the 10th and 21st Panzer Divisions at Sidi-bou-Zid swept away Company A, 701st Tank Destroyer Battalion, along with Combat Command A, 1st Armored Division.[16] On the following day, Company C of the 701st joined the 1st Armored Division's Combat Command C in an incredibly ill-conceived counterattack aimed at recapturing the Sidi-bou-Zid position and was badly battered in the ensuing German ambush.[17]

A damaged Mark VI Tiger tank being inspected by U.S. troops

Elements of the 601st, numbering less than a company, participated in the defense of Sbeitla on 16 February. The tank destroyers were placed in advance of the main defensive position held by Combat Command B, 1st Armored Division. They managed to fire effectively for a while against probing German tanks. Soon, however, German fire proved to be too much for the men of the tank destroyer security sections, who retreated precipitately in their unarmored vehicles. The sight of fleeing security troops unnerved and demoralized the crews of the M-3s. When the tank destroyers attempted to maneuver to new positions under fire, they lost cohesion and were routed.[18]

Although the tank destroyers proved to be unequal to the task of stopping German armor in the open, they eventually did make some important contributions towards staving off Rommel's attack. On 21—22 February, the combined fire of tanks, artillery, and elements of the 601st and 894th Tank Destroyer Battalions halted the westward Axis thrust at Djebel el Hamra.[19]

One month after Kasserine, enemy tanks challenged an intact tank destroyer battalion for the first time. The action took place at El Guettar, where the 601st stood in defense of the 1st Infantry Division's communications and artillery. Except for friendly artillery, the tank destroyers were unsupported. On 23 March, about fifty tanks of the 10th Panzer Division attacked the 601st, which still used the expedient M-3 weapon. A company of the 899th Tank Destroyer Battalion, equipped with M-10s, advanced to reinforce the 601st but was slow in arriving due to traffic and minefields. The tank destroyers, employing the fire-and-movement tactics prescribed by doctrine, turned back the Axis attack and accounted for a reported thirty enemy tanks destroyed. But the victory was dearly bought—about twenty of the twenty-eight M-3s engaged, plus seven of the new M-10s, were lost.[20]

The costly victory at El Guettar stands alone as the only engagement of the North African and Italian campaigns in which a united tank destroyer battalion met and stopped a concerted tank attack. In fact, it was increasingly rare for tank destroyer battalions to be held back in antitank reserve. Battalion commanders noted that the concept "whereby tank destroyer units sat in rear areas awaiting sudden commitment to violent tank action [was] psychologically unsound." Experience showed that if tank destroyers were not on hand when the enemy tank attack started, they were unlikely to arrive in time to influence the outcome.[21] Moreover, attempts to bring the large tank destroyer weapons forward through established positions frequently resulted in the inadvertent destruction of communication wires.[22]

An M-6 tank destroyer in North Africa

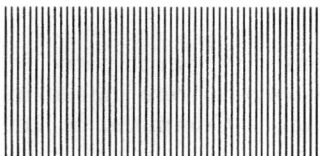

Rather than holding the tank destroyers in reserve, higher commanders in North Africa and Italy tended to distribute tank destroyer battalions to the divisions, where they served to bolster the infantry's inadequate organic antitank defenses. Once attached to a division, the tank destroyer battalion was almost invariably fragmented into companies or even platoons. Reportedly, there was at least one instance of tank destroyers in Tunisia being parceled out singly to rifle platoons.[23] During the Anzio battle in Italy, two tank destroyer platoons were attached to an independent tank battalion that was, in turn, attached to the 45th Division.[24]

Such dispersal proved to be an administrative nightmare. In theory, the flow of logistics for tank destroyer units passed from field army or corps, through the tank destroyer battalion headquarters, to the fighting companies and platoons. In practice, isolated tank destroyer elements often found it difficult to procure such basics as hot food and dental care[25] because neither army, corps, nor battalion could keep track of them. One tank destroyer unit is reported to have requested fuel and ammunition from the division it was attached to and to have received gasoline and 75-mm shells in return. Unfortunately, the M-10 tank destroyer used diesel fuel and three-inch ammunition.[26]

The personnel and maintenance requirements of "orphaned" tank destroyer units frequently went unfulfilled, and weaknesses in leadership often went undetected or uncorrected. All of these problems stemmed from the same cause: tank destroyer elements were not organic to any command, hence no command felt constrained to look after their well-being. Shifting tank destroyer elements from one division to another exacerbated such problems and disrupted the development of tank destroyer teamwork with the other arms, a relationship that was vital to their success on the battlefield.[27]

Typically, tank destroyer companies and platoons attached to infantry formations were sent to the front to supplement the inadequate antitank guns and bazookas of the infantry regiment. With the exception of increasingly rare armored counterthrusts, German tanks, on their part, tended to operate in small numbers and in conjunction with infantry forces, thus making it necessary for tank destroyers to cover wide sections of the front.[28] Like all large weapons, tank destroyers tended to draw enemy artillery fire, making it necessary to dig them into positions located away from the infantry, very often on unfavorable ground.[29] Tank destroyer crews learned the importance of digging good positions, concealing their weapons carefully, and holding fire until enemy tanks came into effective range.[30] Such techniques were more akin to the antitank methods of the Germans and the British than they were to prescribed tank destroyer doctrine. FM 18—5 described tank destroyer action as often taking place after enemy tanks broke through friendly lines,[31] but according to Major General E. M. Harmon, armored division commander in North Africa and Italy, "It is a fixed rule and a point of honor that neither our tanks or tank destroyers will permit their infantry to be overrun by hostile tanks, no matter what it costs to themselves."[32]

Clearly, the battlefield commanders in Tunisia and Italy contravened the most basic principles of tank destroyer doctrine. Instead of maintaining a tank destroyer reserve for defense-in-depth against massed enemy armor, commanders employed tank destroyers in a frontline cordon defense. Considering the diffuse nature of the Axis armored threat, such employment made sense. Adherence to FM 18—5 did not.

Although tank destroyer doctrine held little utility in North Africa and Italy, this is not to suggest that the tank destroyers themselves were useless. In addition to contributing significantly to frontline antitank firepower, tank destroyer battalions, on their own, developed new missions that were not to be found in FM 18—5. The battalion that pioneered the development of secondary missions was apparently the 776th, commanded by Lieutenant Colonel James P. Barney. Barney, like many other tank destroyer officers, was an artilleryman. (Of the traditional arms, Field Artillery felt the closest kinship to the fledgling tank destroyers.) As a gunner, his instincts rebelled at the thought of leaving the battalion's thirty-six tubes idle in the absence of an enemy tank threat. To provide employment for his battalion, Barney worked out techniques and procedures for using tank destroyers as indirect-fire artillery in support of the howitzers of division artillery. Other battalions were quick to emulate the 776th.

Barney divided his three companies into two six-gun batteries, rather than the three four-gun platoons specified in the tables of organization. This restructuring freed some platoon officers to act as observers and produced a battery with approximately the same firepower as a standard battery of four 105-mm howitzers.[33] He then placed each company in support of an artillery battalion. The tank destroyer companies commonly operated their own fire direction centers but, lacking sophisticated equipment, relied on division artillery to help with surveys.[34]

The thirty-six three-inch guns mounted on Barney's M-10s equaled the number of tubes found in three field artillery battalions. Moreover, the three-inch weapons complemented the 105-mm howitzers nicely. They could reach out to fourteen thousand yards—four thousand yards farther than the 105-mm.[35] The three-inch weapon was very accurate, and its shell arrived on target with little warning. The burst radius of the three-inch shell was about equal to that of the 105-mm, but its instantaneous burst reduced the amount of cratering sustained by roads in the path of friendly forces. Moreover, three-inch rounds were cheaper and, being smaller, easier to transport than 105-mm shells. These qualities made the three-inch tank destroyer gun ideal for long-range harassment and interdiction, freeing the artillery's howitzers for close-range missions requiring heavier metal.[36]

The fully tracked M-10 was itself a good gun mount. The tank destroyers could displace and occupy new positions with a minimum of site preparation. Especially when dug in and provided with an improvised turret cover, the M-10 was relatively immune to counterbattery fire. Moreover, the M-10s sought out reverse slopes as artillery positions (to supplement the elevation of the gun), leaving the level ground for towed artillery.[37] In Italy, it was discovered that the M-10 could tow a 105-mm howitzer during displacements, freeing the howitzer's prime mover to haul ammunition and supplies.[38]

But the employment of tank destroyers as reinforcing artillery was not without its drawbacks. Constant firing wore out the high-velocity tubes relatively quickly.[39] Although tank destroyers maintained a basic load of antitank ammunition even when serving as artillery, the secondary mission, nonetheless, interfered with their ability to train for the antitank role. Some battalions split their companies between artillery and antitank missions to maintain a degree of antitank readiness.[40] These drawbacks notwithstanding, battalion commanders agreed that morale improved when tank destroyers were employed in meaningful missions all the time, be they antitank or artillery.[41]

Barney's 776th Tank Destroyer Battalion discovered that when placed well forward in the lines, tank destroyers could fulfill another valuable secondary mission—that of direct-support artillery. Late in the Tunisian campaign, the 776th found itself in support of an attacking tank unit. Prior to the armored assault, the tank destroyers methodically shot up all potential German defensive positions with their powerful three-inch guns. The tanks attacked without loss to antitank guns and discovered that the German defenses had been thoroughly demolished by the destroyers' fire. The 776th built upon this experience and developed a leapfrog technique that allowed the tank destroyers to maintain continuous direct-fire support for advancing friendly elements.[42]

The direct-fire mission was especially important in Italy, where tank destroyers provided covering fire for tanks that, being better armored, closed with and destroyed enemy positions impeding the advance of the foot soldiers. Thus, tank destroyers supported tanks, and tanks supported infantry. During the September 1944 assault on the Gothic Line, specially trained tank destroyer gunners supported the advance by placing rounds through the small gun embrasures of German pillboxes at a range of fifteen hundred yards. Even when openings could not be hit, the high-velocity rounds were quite effective against concrete fortifications.[43] Tank destroyers were so valuable as armored self-propelled assault guns that one battalion in Italy functioned exclusively in the direct-support role for four months.[44]

Ironically, the Tank Destroyer Center at Camp Hood had suggested the use of tank destroyers against fortifications in 1942 but had backed off when accused of overselling the tank destroyer product.[45] The secondary artillery roles, which were developed entirely by units in the combat theaters, proved to be so successful that early in 1943, AGF directed the Unit Training Center at Camp Hood to institute supplemental training in indirect laying.[46]

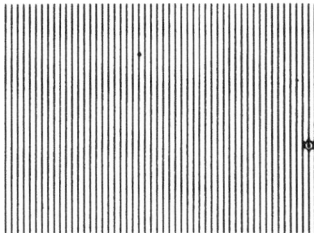

M-10 tank destroyer in Italy

The successes attained in secondary roles did not, however, counteract a growing dissatisfaction with the tank destroyer program as a whole. Commanders at division and lower echelons welcomed the tank destroyers for their versatility and firepower, but higher commanders, as a rule, never reconciled themselves with the concept of an aggressive, offensive antitank arm. Acccording to FM 18—5, "offensive" tank destroyer action took the form of attacking tanks by fire, not by engaging them in "slugging matches."[47] This distinction was too fine, if not downright ambiguous— especially for a field manual. Higher commanders were not alone in failing to differentiate between "offensive action" and "slugging matches," for there were instances in Tunisia of tank destroyers actually charging enemy tanks.[48]

On 21 March 1943, Allied Forces Headquarters (AFHQ—General Eisenhower's theater headquarters for North Africa) issued a training memo that sought to tone down the aggressive orientation of tank destroyer doctrine:

> While it is true that tank destroyer battalions constitute a mobile reserve of antimechanized fire power with which to meet a hostile tank attack, numerous encounters have shown that their characteristics are such as to prohibit their use offensively, either to seek out the hostile tanks in advance of our lines or to meet and shoot it out with them in the open . . . .
>
> The statement in FM 18—5 that they are designed for offensive action will not be construed to the contrary.[49]

Major Allerton Cushman, an observer for AGF and the Tank Destroyer Center who witnessed the Tunisian operation firsthand from December 1942 to March 1943, filed a report bearing similar conclusions. He stated that the M-3 and M-10 tank destroyers

> can not be used offensively to seek out enemy tanks in advance of our lines or to engage in "slugging" matches with them in the open. Any attempt to do so will subject them to destruction by the enemy's AT guns, against which their flat trajectory fire is ineffective.[50]
>
> Troops in Africa have found that the best way to meet a German tank attack is from concealed, dug-in positions with routes reconnoitered to alternate firing positions.[51]
>
> Tank hunting, i.e., dismounted men going out after tanks with sticky grenades, Molotov cocktails, etc., is fine in theory but is considered ridiculous by troops who are in actual war.[52]

Significantly, Cushman found no requirement for a high-speed tank destroyer. He noted that cross-country mobility counted for much more than road speed because the speed of a particular vehicle was seldom reflected by the speed of the unit to which it belonged. Cushman considered the M-10 to be a fine weapon, combining excellent firepower and cross-country mobility with adequate armor protection.[53]

Although both AFHQ and Major Cushman faulted tank destroyer doctrine primarily for its overemphasis on aggressiveness, other officers who took at face value FM 18—5's call for "offensive action" condemned the entire tank destroyer concept. Major General John P. Lucas, a friend of

General Jacob L. Devers

McNair's and Marshall's special observer in Tunisia, reported that *"the Tank Destroyer has, in my opinion, failed to prove its usefullness [sic] . . . I believe that the doctrine_ of an offensive weapon to 'slug it out' with the tank is unsound."* In place of the M-10, he called for a "purely defensive" weapon.[54] All three men who commanded the U.S. II Corps in Tunisia, Major Generals Lloyd R. Fredendall, George S. Patton, and Omar N. Bradley, expressed their dissatisfaction with the aggressive, self-propelled tank destroyer.[55]

General Harmon, who commanded the 2d Armored Division in North Africa, stated flatly that "there is no need for tank destroyers. I believe the whole organization [and] development of the tank destroyer will be a great mistake of the war. Had more powerful guns been installed in American tanks, tank destroyers would have been unnecessary."[56] Lieutenant General Jacob L. Devers, chief of the Armored Force, who toured North Africa in the winter of 1942—43 (and who would one day command AGF), agreed: "The separate tank destroyer arm is not a practical concept on the battlefield. Defensive antitank weapons are essentially artillery. Offensively the weapon to beat the tank is a better tank."[57]

Even the Chief of Staff, General Marshall, who had played a major role in instigating the tank destroyer program, was dissatisfied. His complaint centered on training, rather than doctrine. While in North Africa for the Casablanca Conference of January 1943, he came across a tank destroyer battalion in such a low state of readiness that he was moved to fire off a direct reprimand to General Bruce:

> What I want to draw to your personal attention is that this unit displayed a lack of disciplinary leadership and training that was glaring and meant that it was not useable for any battle against the Germans until it had been reconstituted. The men were all right, the training was seriously wrong ... this is the second time there has come to my attention a deficiency in the ordinary fundamentals of discipline in Tank Destroyer units .... Such procedure is unacceptable to me .... From a superficial point of view it would appear that you have concentrated too much on tactics and technique in comparison with the attention you are giving the fundamentals of discipline.[58]

Bruce satisfied himself that the major fault of the battalion in question was its commander, not its training.[59] However, Bruce's onetime chief of staff agreed with Marshall that training at Camp Hood overemphasized technical training at the expense of discipline.[60] Furthermore, observers reported that tank destroyers, in common with many other elements in the Army, received insufficient training in combined arms prior to combat. This was particularly true for the training conducted at Camp Hood, for it was AGF policy to stress branch training, rather than combined arms training, in the new elements such as armored, tank destroyer, and antiaircraft artillery.[61]

The adverse reports that bombarded Washington and Camp Hood in 1943 contributed to a sharp decline in the power and influence of the tank destroyer establishment. The actual status of the tank destroyers within the Army had never been closely defined, thus the tank destroyer program was particularly vulnerable to the negative recommendations that emanated from officers of high rank and combat experience.

In fact, the institutional status of the tank destroyers had begun to slip even before the North African campaign. The redesignation of the Tank Destroyer Command as the Tank Destroyer Center in August 1942 reflected a sharp restriction of authority. As a center, the tank destroyer facility at Camp Hood was strictly a training establishment, meaning that General Bruce's authority extended no farther than the boundaries of the post. Once a tank destroyer battalion was trained and delivered to a tactical headquarters, it ceased to have any formal connection with the Tank Destroyer Center.[62]

The center itself began to close down some of its training activities as early as October 1943 because the demand for tank destroyers in the theaters of operations was much lower than had been anticipated. In 1941, Bruce had projected an eventual establishment of 220 battalions,[63] but the troop basis for 1943 called for only 144.[64] In the event, only 106 tank destroyer battalions were active by the end of 1943, but even these exceeded demand. Sixty-one battalions participated in the European war, ten sailed to the Pacific theaters, but thirty-five never shipped out at all,[65] having been "rendered surplus by the changing pattern of the war."[66] Eleven of the thirty-five were redesignated as armored field artillery, amphibious tractor, or tank battalions. The remainder were eventually inactivated or broken up for their manpower.[67]

The surviving tank destroyer battalions were much smaller than the original battalions activated in 1942. To alleviate shipping problems, and later a manpower shortage, AGF enforced a policy of reducing the manpower and motor transport in all units.[68] A new tank destroyer table of organization, approved on 27 January 1943, called for 673 men, down from 898. The reduction was accomplished by eliminating the antiaircraft section in each platoon (in accordance with combat experience),[69] combing out administrative and support troops, and combining the nine-man platoon headquarters with the twelve-man security section to form a twelve-man headquarters and security section.[70] Thus, the tank destroyer battalion underwent a manpower reduction of about 25 percent without surrendering any antitank tubes (see figure 7).

As the tank destroyer establishment declined in status and size, it had to fend off attempts to consolidate its diminished functions with those of the other arms. In 1942, General Devers of the Armored Force made an unsuccessful bid to take over tank destroyer training activities. In the fol-

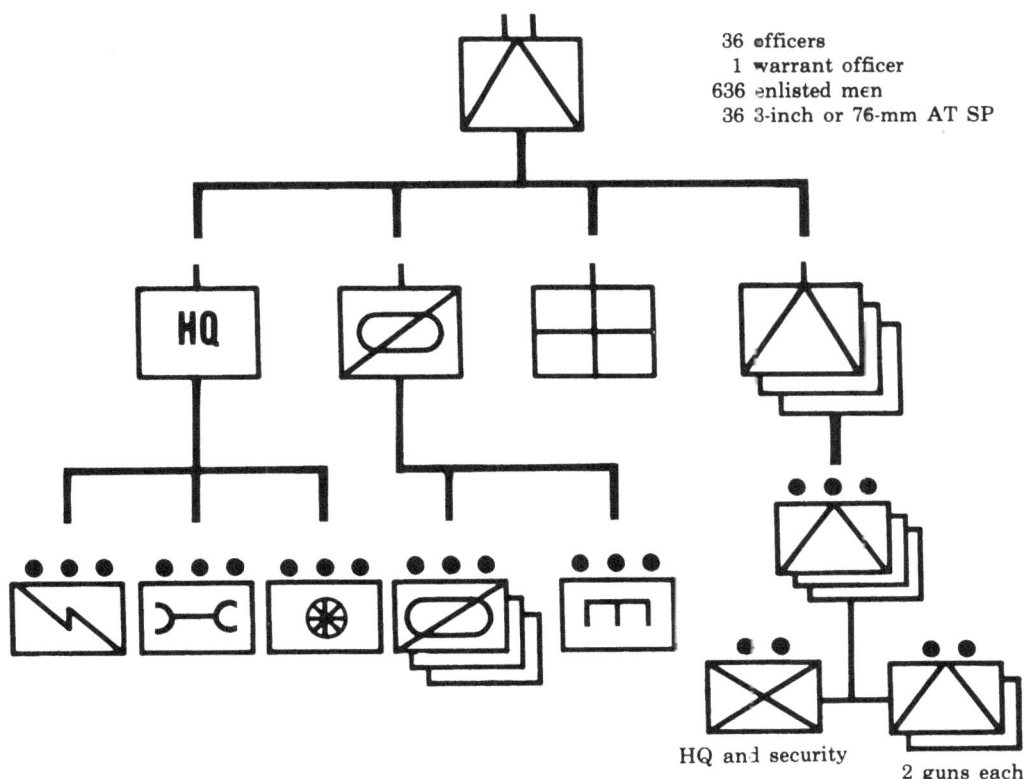

36 officers
1 warrant officer
636 enlisted men
36 3-inch or 76-mm AT SP

HQ and security

2 guns each

Figure 7. Tank destroyer battalion (SP), 1943

lowing year, AGF proposed the assimilation of the tank destroyer arm by the Field Artillery. It took the combined protests of the Tank Destroyer Center and the Field Artillery School to thwart the merger. Even so, Field Artillery became the official branch of all tank destroyer enlisted personnel.[71]

In 1944, the War Department announced a plan to consolidate the Tank Destroyer School with the Armored School, and it did in fact merge the Tank Destroyer Officer Candidate School with that of the Armored Command at Fort Knox. The training activities remaining at Camp Hood were detached from Tank Destroyer Center control and placed directly under the authority of AGF's Replacement and School Command. Even the Tank Destroyer Board was lost to the center when it became an appendage of Headquarters, AGF.[72]

The tank destroyer establishment felt its decline most keenly when it began to lose the freedom to determine and promulgate tank destroyer doctrine. The confusion over "offensive action" that marred tank destroyer operations in Tunisia led AGF to demand that the Tank Destroyer Center rewrite FM 18—5.[73] The work was promptly undertaken, and by May 1943, General Bruce possessed a revision of the original manual that he expected would soon be published. However, over a year would pass before the center, AGF, and the War Department could agree on a new version of FM 18—5.[74]

The leaders of the tank destroyer establishment would not admit that their much maligned doctrine was, in truth, fundamentally flawed. General Bruce claimed that the problems with tank destroyer doctrine were "a misinterpretation of words more than anything else."[75] He explained that the motto—Seek, Strike, and Destroy—had always meant vigorous reconnaissance and destruction of tanks by gunfire, not chasing or charging tanks.[76] Although Bruce continued to believe in the basic tank destroyer concepts, during May 1943 he made a number of important doctrinal concessions. In a significant departure from the original tank destroyer doctrine, Bruce told the instructors of the Tank Destroyer School that "our tank destroyer mission is to *protect* other troops from tank attacks . . . , "[77] whereas FM 18—5 (1942) had stated unequivocally that the mission was the destruction of enemy tanks. Bruce used the same phrase in the cover letter to a Tank Destroyer Center training circular dated 15 May 1943 that was sent to all tank destroyer units for guidance until a revised FM 18—5 appeared. The circular employed the words "aggressive spirit," rather than "offensive action," to describe tank destroyer characteristics. It further stated that "stealth and deception" characterized tank destroyer tactics and warned that tank destroyers were "particularly vulnerable to antitank fire."[78]

Thus, Bruce and the Tank Destroyer Center, under pressure from overseas criticism and from AGF, wrote "offensive action" out of tank destroyer doctrine, but they stood fast on the viability of high-mobility, high-firepower tank destroyers. When AGF ordered the center to begin testing a towed tank destroyer battalion in January 1943, Bruce resisted. General McNair agreed with the veteran commanders of the Tunisian campaign that at least some battalions should be armed with the more easily concealed towed gun, but in the eyes of the tank destroyer establishment, the self-propelled gun remained the centerpiece of doctrine. The specially designed M-18, upon which the hopes of tank destroyer advocates rested, was still a year away from full production.

Bruce's objections proved futile and on 31 March 1943, AGF ordered the conversion of fifteen battalions then in training at Camp Hood from self-propelled to towed. Eventually, AGF ordered that half of all tank destroyer battalions adopt the towed gun.[79] A table of organization for the towed battalion became official on 7 May 1943. It was similar to that of the self-propelled battalion except that there was no reconnaissance company; instead, two reconnaissance platoons were placed in the battalion headquarters company. The need for larger gun crews and more security troops raised the battalion's complement to 816 officers and men.[80] Ordnance quickly produced a version of the three-inch gun, towed by a half-track troop carrier, to arm the new battalions (see figure 8).[81]

The towed tank destroyer battalion demonstrated significant drawbacks almost immediately. Instructors at Camp Hood found that towed units required a completely new program of tactical and technical instruction.[82] When towed battalions first entered combat in Italy, they compared unfavorably to self-propelled tank destroyers. Battalion commanders generally

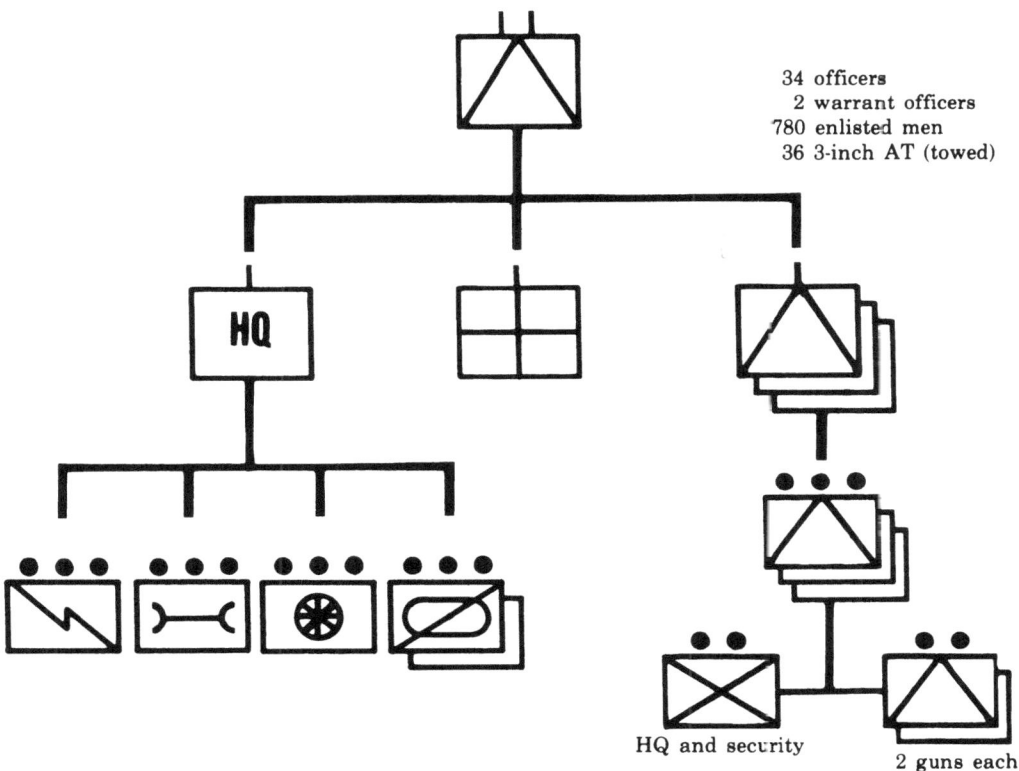

34 officers
2 warrant officers
780 enlisted men
36 3-inch AT (towed)

HQ

HQ and security

2 guns each

Figure 8. Tank destroyer battalion (towed), 1943

agreed that the towed gun was easier to conceal than the M-10 or M-18 but found that it was harder to man and fire in the forward areas and that it was not readily adaptable to the secondary missions that made self-propelled tank destroyers so valuable.[83] The towed gun was simply a less versatile weapon, and it appeared at a time when the versatility of the self-propelled tank destroyer was one of the few bright spots of the entire program.

Ironically, the day of the towed antitank gun was passing on all fronts of the European war. The difficulty of concealing the self-propelled tank destroyer in the open terrain of North Africa, which had generated many calls for towed guns, was not common to Italy or western Europe. In the east, both the German and Soviet Armies were turning to self-propelled anti-tank guns in increasing numbers, even as the U.S. Army adopted towed tank destroyers.

In sum, the advent of the towed tank destroyer did nothing to resuscitate the declining tank destroyer establishment. The credibility of the tank destroyer program had been badly and permanently tarnished by adverse reaction to a doctrine predicated on inaccurate notions of armored warfare and flawed by a dangerous and unwarranted advocacy of "offensive" tactics. An apologist could claim that the tank destroyer concept had yet to be fairly tested, given the piecemeal employment of German armor, the use of expedient tank destroyer equipment, and the supposed misuse of tank destroyers by higher commanders. However, it must be noted that enemy tanks were present in both Tunisia and Italy, and that tank destroyers alone failed to nullify them, in part because tank destroyer doctrine lacked the flexibility to provide for unanticipated circumstances. Thus, doctrine was largely abandoned, and the rationale underlying the existence of a tank destroyer arm brought into question.

The Tank Destroyer Center and Headquarters, AGF, were islands of faith surrounded by seas of doubt. With the departure of General Bruce to assume command of the 77th Division in May 1943 and the tragic death of General McNair in July 1944, the tank destroyer establishment lost its strongest advocates. The future of tank destroyers in the U.S. Army would hinge upon their performance in the invasion of northwest Europe, scheduled for 1944. The invasion would bring the Allies face-to-face with the masters of blitzkrieg in the decisive campaign of the war.

The European Theater:
A Pyrrhic Victory

The tank destroyers that fought in the climactic campaigns of World War II operated under an official doctrine much changed since 1942 and the days of Seek, Strike, and Destroy. On 18 July 1944, more than a year after AGF directed the Tank Destroyer Center to revise its doctrine, the War Department published a completely new edition of FM 18—5 entitled *Tactical Employment, Tank Destroyer Unit.* The new manual covered the tank destroyer battalion and company and was accompanied by four smaller manuals that dealt individually with the self-propelled tank destroyer platoon, the towed platoon, the reconnaissance platoon, and the pioneer platoon.[1]

The changes in tank destroyer doctrine were much more than organizational in nature. The new manuals incorporated a number of revisions that reflected the battlefield lessons of North Africa and Italy. For example, the 1944 version of FM 18—5 made no reference to Seek, Strike, and Destroy or to "offensive" tank destroyer tactics. Instead, it indicated that the "action of tank destroyers is characterized by an aggressive spirit . . . . They employ stealth and deception in opening fire."[2] Also, *"Tank destroyers ambush hostile tanks but do not charge or chase them."*[3]

Tactical mobility, once the keystone of the tank destroyer concept, was also de-emphasized in FM 18—5 (1944). Whereas the 1942 manual had indicated that mobility, rather than heavy armor, would protect the tank destroyer from enemy fire, the 1944 edition stressed the use of cover and concealment to compensate for the acknowledged "vulnerability of tank destroyers to hostile tank, antitank, and artillery fire."[4] Tank destroyers were advised to fight from their primary firing positions until those positions became untenable,[5] rather than automatically shifting to alternate positions after firing three or four rounds, as FM 18—5 (1942) had suggested.[6] This change was in keeping with General McNair's belief that tanks were best fought "by sticking, not maneuvering."[7]

To compensate for the new restrictions placed on maneuver, the 1944 manual called for the positioning of tank destroyers in depth, in a manner reminiscent both of the prewar antitank box and of antitank techniques employed by the Germans in North Africa. Specifically, FM 18—5 (1944) recommended that the tank destroyer company commander position two of his platoons forward and one to the rear and that only one platoon (sometimes the rear one) open fire first, with the other two remaining silent until the enemy made himself vulnerable by maneuvering against the active guns.[8]

FM 18—5 (1944) made no reference to the "semi-independent" nature of tank destroyer operations but rather laid increased emphasis on combined arms: "[Tank destroyers] are not capable of independent action, hence they cooperate closely with other troops."[9] The new manual made clear that since enemy tanks would often be strongly supported by infantry, tank destroyers should be near, or with, friendly infantry whose plans and dispositions were known to the tank destroyers.[10] "The tank destroyer commander takes advantage of infantry dispositions to protect [his tank destroyers] against enemy infantry. In turn, the tank destroyer guns help protect the infantry."[11] Another indication of the shift away from the semi-independent operations postulated in 1942 was the dramatic increase in the amount of text devoted to the subject of operations conducted directly under division or corps control—twenty-two pages in FM 18—5 (1944) as opposed to only five in the 1942 edition.

FM 18—5 (1944) expanded slightly upon the secondary missions that tank destroyers were capable of executing when not confronted by enemy armor. Among the missions discussed were those of direct and indirect artillery, roving artillery, pillbox destruction, and direct support of infantry.[12] The new manual also offered some helpful guidance on tying tank destroyer companies in to field artillery units for employment in the artillery role.[13]

In North Africa and Italy, the extensive employment of tank destroyers in secondary missions had predisposed higher commanders to fragment tank destroyer units and to detach elements from their battalions. FM 18—5 (1944) suggested that tank destroyer battalions should be employed intact[14] but also conceded that fragmentation would occur during secondary missions[15] and when the enemy used his armor locally in small-scale operations, necessitating the distribution of tank destroyers among the forward lines.[16]

The towed tank destroyer, with characteristics differing radically from those of the self-propelled weapon, had required different methods of employment on the battlefields of Italy. Accordingly, the 1944 manuals provided the towed tank destroyer with what amounted to a separate doctrine. The towed platoon merited a field manual (FM 18—21) similar to, but distinct from, the manual for the self-propelled platoon (FM 18—20). FM 18—5 (1944) treated the towed company and battalion concurrently with their self-propelled counterparts but suggested methods of employing the towed units that allowed for their lesser mobility and greater vulnerability: towed guns were declared to be unsuitable for use in isolated outposts; towed tank destroyers were more likely to be pre-positioned and left in position once sited; and towed battalions would generally be employed to reinforce the organic antitank guns of a host division and in such a role would engage enemy tanks within the area occupied by friendly infantry.[17] (The planners for the

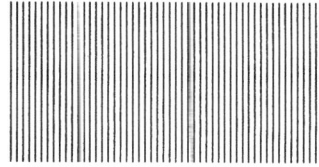

The three-inch towed
tank destroyer with its
prime mover

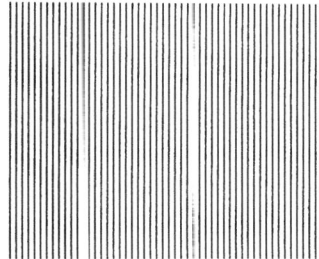

Normandy invasion would make the towed – self-propelled dichotomy complete by assigning towed battalions to each infantry division and retaining the self-propelled battalions under higher echelons for employment in the vintage tank destroyer role.)[18]

As the foregoing examples demonstrate, FM 18—5 (1944) incorporated a number of the doctrinal modifications that tank destroyer units had developed in battle and was thus more realistic in tone and content than the 1942 edition it replaced. Taken as a group, these modifications brought tank destroyer doctrine into closer conformity with the purely defensive doctrine developed by the Infantry for the antitank elements organic to the infantry battalion and regiment.[19] Both doctrines stressed "sticking" rather than maneuvering, the use of cover and concealment, and close coordination with the rifle elements.

In other respects, however, FM 18—5 (1944) adhered doggedly to the original, unproven, tank destroyer concept. In 1943, General Bruce had indicated that the mission of tank destroyers was the protection of friendly forces from enemy tanks, but the 1944 manual returned to the original idea that the "primary mission of tank destroyer units is the destruction of hostile tanks by direct gunfire."[20] Moreover, FM 18—5 (1944) perpetuated the notion that massed tanks constituted the primary threat, and that tank destroyers should respond by massing into large units that would travel at high speeds to intercept the armored penetration behind friendly lines.[21] The new field manual retained a section on tank destroyer groups (and even brigades) despite the fact that only one group headquarters had seen combat to date, and that group had served merely to relay orders from the division to tank destroyer battalions.[22]

It is true that the concern with massed tanks exhibited in FM 18—5 (1944) was not substantiated by combat experience in Tunisia and Italy, but it was in accordance with the widely held belief that the liberation of Europe would provoke the Germans into the massed employment of armor on a large scale. British General Bernard L. Montgomery, commander of Allied ground forces for the invasion of Normandy, drew up a plan of operations that postulated significant armored action by both sides early in the campaign. Allied intelligence accurately estimated that the German forces in western Europe included ten panzer divisions, all of which could reach the Allied beachhead within five days of the first landings. Montgomery correctly assumed that Field Marshal Rommel, the German commander charged with defending the coast, planned to launch those panzer divisions in heavy attacks aimed at breaking up the beachheads before the Allies could consolidate their positions. To forestall the Germans and retain the initiative, Montgomery's plan called for Allied armored thrusts designed to seize key terrain and keep Rommel's forces off-balance.[23]

These cut-and-thrust sallies on the part of major armored formations promised much work for the tank destroyers. Original planning estimates allocated a total of seventy-two tank destroyer battalions to the European theater (a figure later reduced by about twenty), half of which were to be towed and half to be self-propelled. The actual invasion forces that sailed for Normandy included eleven towed and nineteen self-propelled battalions, although only one of the towed battalions landed with the assault elements, owing to the vulnerability of the towed weapons system during amphibious operations. As noted earlier, towed battalions were attached directly to infantry divisions, while self-propelled battalions were retained in reserve under group headquarters at the corps and army echelons.[24] Ultimately, fifty-six tank destroyer battalions, thirteen group headquarters, and one brigade headquarters would see service in the European theater,[25] with tank destroyer personnel accounting for roughly 6 percent of the manpower making up the four field armies in the theater.[26]

On the basis of tank destroyer numbers, it would seem that the American forces in Europe should have been adequately protected from the German panzers, even given the massive armored assaults that the Germans were expected to launch against the Allies. In terms of weapons capabilities, the future looked equally bright. Ordnance tests indicated that tank destroyer guns would be able to penetrate the frontal armor of the massive Mark VI Tiger tank at a comfortable two thousand yards.[27] Prior to the invasion, the headquarters of the European Theater of Operations, in response to a query from AGF about the need for a more powerfully armed tank destroyer, indicated that the existing weapons would be adequate.[28] Even the armored units preparing for the invasion, including veterans of Tunisia, were satisfied with the current version of the M-4 tank, which carried a short, general-purpose 75-mm gun.[29]

Unfortunately, the ordnance tests were in error, and the confidence residing in tank and tank destroyer armament was misplaced. American troops in Normandy would find themselves unexpectedly vulnerable to the

German panzers. Events would prove that no tank destroyer could reliably stop a Tiger at any more than fifty yards.[30] The Mark V Panther was not much easier to destroy. Firing tests conducted in Normandy, utilizing actual Panther hulks, were to demonstrate that only the 90-mm antiaircraft gun and the 105-mm howitzer, firing shaped charges, could penetrate the Panther's frontal armor with any regularity.[31] To destroy a Panther, a tank destroyer with a three-inch or 76-mm gun would have to aim for the side

The German Mark V
Panther tank

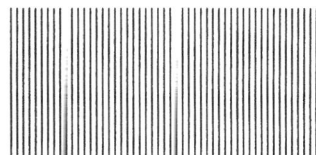

or rear of the turret, the opening through which the hull-mounted machine gun projected, or for the underside of the gun shield (which would occasionally deflect the round downwards into the top deck of the tank).[32] Moreover, the Tiger's superb 88-mm gun and the Panther's high-velocity 75-mm piece could destroy any American armored vehicle with ease. The lapse in technological planning that sent American tanks and tank destroyers into Europe with inadequate armament occurred despite the fact that American troops in the Mediterranean theater had been fighting both the Tiger and the Panther since 1943.

Almost by accident, a remedy was at hand. In 1942, the Ordnance Department on its own initiative (and against the wishes of the Tank Destroyer Center, which disapproved of expedients) experimentally mounted a 90-mm antiaircraft gun in the modified turret of an M-10 tank destroyer. The design was standardized as the M-36 in June 1944.[33] On 6 July, exactly one month after the Normandy landings and less than two months after assuring AGF that the existing tank destroyers were adequate, the European Theater of Operations requested that all battalions equipped with the M-10 be converted to the M-36.[34]

The M-36 would not arrive in Europe until September 1944, but once it reached the front, it proved to be the only American armored vehicle that could match the heavier German tanks in firepower. One M-36 destroyed a Panther with one round at a range of 3,200 yards,[35] and another fired five rounds at a tank 4,600 yards distant, scored two hits, and disabled the tank.[36] The M-36 was equally impressive in the secondary missions. In the direct-fire role, a 90-mm armor-piercing shell could penetrate 4.5 feet of non-

The M-36 tank destroyer
with 90-mm gun

reinforced concrete,[37] while in the indirect-fire mission, the M-36 could throw a projectile 19,000 yards.[38]

Until the M-36 arrived in quantity, however, the M-10 and M-18 constituted the best available antitank weapons in the American arsenal. Crews spoke highly of the M-10, despite its firepower disadvantage, calling it "a great weapon." They especially admired the M-10 for its versatility and for the reliability of its twin diesel engines, although they felt that it would be improved by the addition of a power-traverse turret, a machine gun mounted for employment against ground targets, and a turret cover for protection against small-arms fire. Some crews created improvised turret covers, removed the antiaircraft machine gun from the rear of the turret, and remounted it facing forward.[39]

British troops also used a version of the M-10, called the Achilles, that mounted a 17-pounder gun and with which they were extremely satisfied. The British recognized, though, that even with the high-velocity 17-pounder, "it [was] suicide deliberately to try to engage in a battle of fire and movement with an enemy tank."[40]

Tank destroyer crews spoke highly of the M-18 as well. The M-18, with its 76-mm gun, was equal to the M-10 in firepower, was more mobile, but it carried less armor. One observer in Europe noted that the First Army placed more value on frontal armor than on speed and thus preferred M-10 battalions. On the other hand, the freewheeling Third Army valued the M-18 for its extraordinary mobility, which even enabled it to accompany cavalry units on reconnaissance missions.[41]

Notwithstanding the praise of tank destroyer crews, the fact remained that once landed in Normandy, the tank destroyers found it highly inadvisable to react aggressively to enemy armor, even though every German tank encountered was by no means a Panther or a Tiger. Fortunately, the full-blooded panzer counterattack against the beachhead never materialized, for reasons that included divisiveness in the German high command, Allied deception measures, French Resistance activities, and Allied control of the air. The Germans opted instead for a strategy of attrition, whereby they "roped in" the beachhead with a static defense-in-depth. Thus, the major problem confronting American troops in Normandy was not the staving off of massed tanks but rather the rooting out of a stubborn, entrenched enemy.

The terrain in Normandy is dominated by hedgerows—banks of earth and tangled vegetation bounding every field—that the Germans converted into a maze of defensive positions. There, American infantry elements were bled white in fighting reminiscent of World War I at its worst. The foot troops desperately needed armored support to facilitate their advance. According to Army doctrine, this support should have come from independent tank battalions attached to the divisions at need, but there were not enough tank battalions to go around. In the European theater there were, ultimately, only thirty-seven such battalions, whereas there were forty-seven infantry and armored divisions,[42] all of which needed additional support.

As a consequence, very early in the Normandy campaign, tank destroyers were once more sent directly to the front to fill a void in firepower. Under the prevailing tactical conditions, towed tank destroyers proved to be of little use. They could not fire over the hedgerows, could not be pushed up among the forward positions, and could not displace once they disclosed their positions. Among the tank destroyer battalions assigned to First Army during the Normandy fighting, towed battalions on the average accounted for 5.8 enemy tanks and 4.0 pillboxes each, whereas the average self-propelled battalion in Normandy destroyed 22.5 panzers and 23.2 pillboxes.[43]

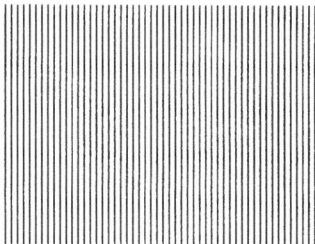

An M-10 tank destroyer in Normandy

Infantry riding an M-10
after the breakout from
Normandy

Of necessity, the self-propelled battalions held in corps reserve were sent to the front and attached to divisions. These battalions theoretically remained a part of the corps tank destroyer pool, but in practice, their attachment to the respective divisions became virtually permanent. Long-term attachment facilitated the development of teamwork and confidence between the tank destroyers and the other arms, which prompted tank destroyer officers to observe that the self-propelled battalions should have been made organic to the divisions from the outset, so that training and familiarization could have been accomplished *prior* to combat.[44]

Once attached to a division, the tank destroyer battalion was typically assigned by companies to the infantry regiments, whereupon the regiments generally assigned a tank destroyer platoon to each battalion. Under these circumstances, tank destroyer doctrine was fundamentally unworkable and justifiably abandoned.

The primary task of the tank destroyer became infantry support. When the infantry attacked, tank destroyers would roll with the advance some five hundred to eight hundred yards behind the assault elements, shooting up all potential enemy positions in the path of the infantry. The infantry, in turn, neutralized antitank positions that threatened the tank destroyer.[45] The armor on the M-10 and M-18 tank destroyers was adequate to protect their crews from small-arms fire, and the high velocity and flat trajectory of their guns made them very effective against enemy strongpoints. The presence of rapid-firing tank destroyers noticeably eroded enemy morale and bolstered that of the assaulting infantry.[46]

In the course of heavy fighting around Saint Lô, the 654th Tank Destroyer Battalion and the 35th Division to which it was attached developed an especially effective technique for penetrating hedgerow defenses. One platoon of four M-10s was assigned to each regimental sector, where engineers blew gaps in the hedgerows to bring the tank destroyers up to the front line of infantry. Tank destroyer observers, on foot with the infantry, guided the M-10s into position and directed their fire onto enemy machine-gun nests in the hedgerow to the front. With enemy fire thus suppressed, the infantry attacked and cleared the enemy hedgerow. Engineers then opened paths to bring the tank destroyers forward again to repeat the process against the next hedgerow.[47]

Following the breakout from Normandy and the race to the German frontier, tank destroyers replayed their success in direct support missions, but this time American troops confronted the interlocking fortifications of the Westwall (known to the Allies as the Siegfried Line), rather than hedgerows. From a range of one thousand yards, ten rounds from a tank destroyer gun would penetrate a small pillbox or jam the shutters of a larger work and would often cause the pillbox crew to surrender. The penetrative effect of tank destroyer fire was enhanced by aiming all four guns of a platoon at the same point and firing simultaneously. The 629th Tank Destroyer Battalion (M-10) discovered that the easiest way to reduce a pillbox was from the rear—where one three-inch round would blow in the entrance and one high-explosive round sent through the open doorway invariably induced the survivors to surrender.[48]

The 803d Tank Destroyer Battalion supported infantry in the reduction of Westwall fortifications by assigning a platoon of four M-10s to each infantry assault battalion and providing the tank destroyers with infantry radios so they could be controlled by the infantry company commanders. The tank destroyer platoon then engaged a pair of pillboxes at a time, with one M-10 firing at the embrasure of each pillbox, and with two M-10s standing by in an overwatch role. The three-inch rounds did not usually penetrate the fortifications, but they did prevent the enemy from manning

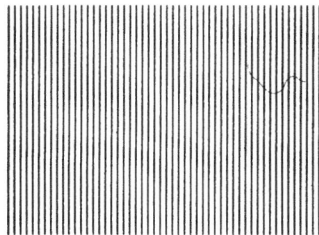

An M-10 firing as artillery

his weapons, thus enabling the American infantry to reach the blind side of the fortifications. On a radio signal from the infantry company, the tank destroyers ceased fire, and the infantry assaulted the pillboxes.[49]

Tank destroyers not employed in the front lines often found themselves providing indirect fire in support of division or corps artillery. Prior to the invasion, battalions received the training and equipment that enabled them to conduct basic surveys and perform fire direction without outside help. In the course of the fighting in Normandy, 87 percent of the ammunition expended by self-propelled tank destroyers in VIII Corps was fired in indirect missions. VIII Corps' towed tank destroyers, unemployable in direct-support roles, fired 98 percent of their ammunition as indirect-fire artillery.[50]

An outstanding example of tank destroyers employed as artillery occurred in February 1945, when XIX Corps mounted a set-piece two-division assault across the Roer River. XIX Corps called upon the 702d (M-36) and 801st (towed) Tank Destroyer Battalions, under the control of the 2d Tank Destroyer Group, to reinforce the fire of division and corps artillery. When the crossing began, the towed tank destroyer battalion placed neutralization fire on all known German positions in the assault sector, and three of the M-36 platoons delivered interdiction fire at the rate of one hundred rounds per platoon per hour on three highways leading to the crossing area. Meanwhile, the other six M-36 platoons provided direct fire on call from tank destroyer observers who crossed the river with the infantry. When the assault elements passed beyond effective direct-fire range, these platoons also shifted to indirect fire. After three and one-half hours of planned fires, the tank destroyers became available for on-call fire missions designated by a tank destroyer fire direction center collocated with the corps fire direction center. Missions included interdiction, harassment, and neutralization fires. The tank destroyers were prepared (but not called upon) to execute "time on target" fires, rather sophisticated procedures that would result in the shells from every gun arriving on the target at the same time.[51]

The extensive use of tank destroyers in secondary missions invoked certain penalties that were all too familiar to the veterans of Tunisia. Tank destroyers sent to the front lines quickly drew heavy German artillery and mortar fire upon themselves and upon the adjacent infantry. Tank destroyer crews in forward positions found it necessary to strap sandbags onto their vehicles as protection against German "bazooka" rounds.[52] Some infantry commanders preferred to use tanks rather than tank destroyers in the immediate front lines because snipers and hand grenades took a heavy toll among the crews of the open-topped tank destroyers.[53] Unfortunately, other infantry officers were unaware of tank destroyer limitations and attempted to employ tank destroyers exactly as they would use the better-armored tanks.[54] Overall, tank destroyers "misused" in this manner suffered greater losses and obtained less-impressive results than units in which the tank destroyer commanders were encouraged to exercise judgement and initiative.[55]

Even though tank destroyer doctrine and occasional directives from higher headquarters urged that tank destroyer battalions be used as units,[56]

M-10 tank destroyers carrying sandbags to augment their armor

the long-term employment of tank destroyers in secondary missions inevitably resulted in the chronic fragmentation of tank destroyer elements. With tank destroyer companies attached to each infantry regiment or armored combat command, and with tank destroyer platoons often distributed among infantry battalions and armored task forces, the tank destroyer battalion headquarters lost all tactical control over its fighting elements. Frequently, the battalion even surrendered control over supply and administration to the host units, which were not always capable of looking after the tank destroyer elements.[57] Early in the European campaign, battalion headquarters were careful to maintain contact with their tank destroyer companies and to develop contingency plans for reconcentrating the battalion in case of a major panzer attack. As the campaign progressed, the tank destroyer battalion commanders realized that their companies were not likely to be returned to them, particularly not in times of crises, when the frontline troops would need all available support. Gradually, contingency planning ceased, and the tank destroyer battalion headquarters became, for tactical purposes, largely superfluous.[58]

The tank destroyer group headquarters attached to each corps was also intended to be a tactical headquarters and, as such, had even less to do than the battalion. (The role played by the 2d Tank Destroyer Group in the Roer River crossing was a rare exception.) Of thirteen group headquarters sent to the European theater, nine functioned primarily as corps-level special staff sections for antitank affairs. Other functions that tank destroyer group headquarters performed at various times included supervision of antiairborne forces, command of corps rest centers, coordination of corps headquarters security forces, and protection of communication lines.[59] The one tank destroyer brigade sent to Europe was attached to Third Army, where it served as a task force headquarters on one occasion and spent the rest of the war as Third Army's antitank section.[60] In other field army headquarters, tank destroyers fell under the artillery sections for planning and administrative purposes.

Extensive employment as assault guns and indirect-fire artillery did not excuse the tank destroyers from their primary mission of destroying enemy armor. Even though the German panzers in western Europe generally fought in small numbers and were limited to shallow penetrations in conjunction with infantry operations, the American infantry remained terribly vulnerable to tank attack. By 1944, the 57-mm antitank gun had replaced the 37-mm in the infantry battalion antitank platoon and regimental antitank company, but this weapon was as inadequate in 1944 as the 37-mm gun had been in 1942. Predictably, tank destroyers were again called upon to provide frontline antitank defense for the infantry divisions. This mission bore relatively little relation to the doctrine concerning massed tanks described in FM 18—5; rather, it merged imperceptibly with the direct-support mission. Close cooperation with infantry facilitated mutual support among the arms, but it also meant that tank destroyers assigned to infantry support did not enjoy the luxury of choosing ideal terrain upon which to meet enemy armor when called upon to perform the antitank mission. According to one battalion commander,

> Often the TD cannot remain on the reverse slope of a hill and let the [enemy] tanks come to them [sic]. It may be necessary for the infantry to organize their positions on a forward slope. No infantry commander is going to allow tanks to run over his men if he has any way of driving them off. The TDs will be ordered out on the forward slope to take the oncoming tanks under direct fire. This must be done even in the face of what seems certain destruction for men and vehicles.[61]

When given the option, tank destroyers chose to ambush tanks from positions that provided flank shots and to fight it out in place, for it was "far more dangerous to withdraw or to move forward than to fight in position when attacked by armor."[62] Experienced tank destroyers never fought alone but always in pairs or more; conversely, they refused to be "suckered in" by a "lone" German tank, for there was usually another lurking nearby.[63]

On several rare but noteworthy occasions, the Germans broke with their policy of small-scale armored operations and massed their tanks for large-scale attacks. These attacks came unexpectedly and invariably caught the tank destroyers in a dispersed state. In no case were tank destroyers able to mass into groups or brigades as prescribed by doctrine. Inasmuch as they possessed the best available antitank guns, tank destroyers, nonetheless, played an important part in stopping the panzers each time they came out in force.

On 7 August 1944, elements of three understrength panzer divisions and one *panzergrenadier* (mechanized infantry) division launched an attack at Mortain, France, aimed at cutting off the American forces breaking out of the Normandy beachhead. The brunt of the attack fell upon the 30th Infantry Division, with the 823d Tank Destroyer Battalion (towed) attached. The guns of the 823d had been hastily sited and were not in mutually supporting positions. Some platoons were without infantry support. First, the defenders fought off an infantry attack and then an assault mounted by panzers accompanied by infantry. The tank destroyers fought stubbornly but without coordination, for all of the 823d's fighting elements had been parceled out to the regiments, and tactical control was in the hands of the infantry commanders. Those tank destroyers supported by other arms did well; those not supported were quickly overrun. Companies A and B, 823d Tank Destroyer Battalion, received the Presidential Unit Citation for the part they played in stopping the Mortain counterattack, but the cost had come high, prompting the 823d to train its gun crews to fire the three-inch weapon with two or three men, freeing the remainder of the crew to fight off enemy infantry.[64]

One month later, Third Army's crossing of the Moselle River and capture of Nancy provoked another German counterattack that involved significant panzer elements. Combat Command A of the 4th Armored Division, with Company C, 704th Tank Destroyer Battalion (M-18) attached, occupied an exposed position at Arracourt, when it was attacked by the 113th Panzer Brigade on 19 September. Heavy fog blanketed the area, which aided the Germans in gaining surprise, but which also negated the superior range of German tank armament. On the other hand, the nimble M-18 was at its best at Arracourt. The tank destroyers were able to maneuver quickly on the muddy, rough ground, giving them the opportunity to seize commanding terrain and occupy successive firing positions in the path of the panzers. One tank destroyer platoon claimed the destruction of fifteen enemy tanks, although three of its four M-18s were put out of action.[65]

The supreme test of the tank destroyer forces in Europe came in December 1944 when German Army Group B launched a full-scale offensive through the Ardennes—the scene of the great blitzkrieg of 1940. Ten panzer divisions were among the twenty-four German divisions that shattered the overextended lines of U.S. First Army. According to doctrine, First Army's tank destroyer battalions should have formed up into groups, raced to the scene of the attack, and ambushed the panzer spearheads. But, of course, the tank destroyers were dispersed beyond recall, and with hundreds of panzers on the loose, their host divisions were most unlikely to release them. Moreover, with the roads clogged by retreating American units, it seems unlikely that massed tank destroyers could have played out the "fire brigade" scenario in any case. The Americans actually stopped the German onslaught by denying transportation chokepoints to the enemy and separating the panzer spearheads from their follow-on elements, and not by ambushing the panzer spearheads themselves, as tank destroyer doctrine would suggest. By and large, the two dozen tank destroyer battalions that participated significantly in the Ardennes campaign fought in small units and in relatively static, defensive roles.

Two towed tank destroyer battalions in the center of the American line were among the first units to feel the weight of the German attack. The 820th, attached to the ill-fated 106th Infantry Division, was unable to put up much of a fight. The Germans overran one entire company because the towed guns could not be hitched up and removed from danger. Other elements fell back to Saint-Vith and participated in the defensive battle fought there.[66] The 28th Infantry Division's attached tank destroyer battalion, the 630th, also had elements deployed in the path of the initial German onslaught. By companies and platoons, the 630th added its fire to the desperate delaying actions in which the 28th Division sacrificed itself to buy time for the reinforcement of Bastogne. Three days of fighting reduced the 630th to the battalion headquarters and one company without guns.[67]

On the northern shoulder of the German breakthrough, the 99th and 2d Infantry Divisions, with the aid of a number of tank destroyer elements, defended a vital terrain feature known as Elsenborn Ridge against repeated heavy assaults. The Germans attacked in company-size task forces consisting of both panzers and infantry. The defenders responded by first breaking up the enemy formations with artillery fire and then striking them from the flanks with tank and tank destroyer fire. The fighting surged back and forth through villages and rough terrain, a circumstance that provided ample opportunities for tank destroyer ambushes and cut ranges down to as little as twenty-five yards. One company of the 644th Tank Destroyer Battalion (M-10) destroyed seventeen tanks with the loss of two tank destroyers. Towed tank destroyers, being unable to maneuver for flank shots or to evade enemy thrusts, fared less well at Elsenborn. The 801st Tank Destroyer Battalion (towed) lost seventeen guns and sixteen half-track prime movers in two days because the guns bogged down in the mud and fell easy prey to German artillery and infantry.[68]

The stubborn American defense of two crossroad towns in the throat of the German advance, Saint-Vith and Bastogne, disrupted the German offensive with fatal results. Elements of three tank destroyer battalions, including some M-36s, participated in the 7th Armored Division's epic battle at Saint-Vith. The tank destroyers provided a powerful base of fire for the hard-pressed defenders, with the M-36 proving to be especially valuable as a "sure kill" against enemy armor.[69] At Bastogne, it was the 705th Tank

A Third Army M-36 in Metz during the autumn campaign of 1944

The three-inch towed tank destroyer was difficult to manhandle

Destroyer Battalion (M-18) that bolstered the fragile perimeter held by the soldiers of the 101st Airborne Division.[70]

Tank destroyers emerged from the Ardennes campaign with a mixed reputation. On the positive side of the ledger, statisticians credited the tank destroyer battalions with the destruction of 306 enemy tanks.[71] Many of these kills came during the decisive engagements of the campaign. On the negative side, the towed tank destroyer had proved to be a failure. Whereas self-propelled tank destroyers scored the most kills, towed battalions suffered the heavier losses: in the first critical week of the campaign, First Army lost seventy-seven tank destroyers, sixty-five of which were towed.[72] At five thousand pounds, the towed three-inch gun was five times heavier than the old 37-mm gun, was extremely difficult to manhandle, proved highly vulnerable to all enemy fire, and still could not destroy enemy tanks with certainty. Any lingering support for the towed tank destroyer evaporated in the chaos of the Ardennes campaign, following which all towed battalions were scheduled for conversion to self-propelled weapons.[73]

It must also be noted that of the self-propelled tank destroyers, only the M-36 had shown itself to be wholly satisfactory in terms of firepower, and even the M-36 suffered the disadvantages of thin armor and an open turret, a fault common to all self-propelled tank destroyers. After the Ardennes campaign, M-10 battalions began exchanging their weapons for the M-36.[74] Ordnance developed overhead armor for tank destroyer turrets[75] that, when taken together with the common practice of sandbagging tank destroyers to augment their armor, made the tank destroyer more like a tank than like the weapon initially envisaged by General Bruce. In the minds of higher commanders, tanks and tank destroyers became increasingly interchangeable as the European war drew to a close.

The same was true in the Pacific theater, where tank employment and tank destroyer employment were essentially identical. Because of the minimal threat posed by Japanese tanks, the three tank destroyer battalions that saw combat in the Philippines operated almost exclusively as assault guns and supporting artillery.[76] In preparation for the invasion of Japan, the Tank Destroyer Center at Camp Hood turned away from the problems of killing tanks and devoted its experimental efforts instead to the use of tank destroyers in reducing Japanese-style fortifications.[77] The battalions scheduled to participate in the invasion considered their tank destroyers to be tanks in every way, save for their open turrets.[78]

As the distinction between tank and tank destroyer faded, the only advantage that the tank destroyer could claim over the tank was the superior firepower of the M-36. In February 1945, even that advantage disappeared when the first M-26 heavy tanks arrived in the European theater. The M-26 mounted the same 90-mm gun as the M-36 tank destroyer and was, of course, better armored. It is true that tank destroyers, especially the M-18, retained an edge over the tank in terms of mobility, but by the end of the war, American soldiers, for the most part, preferred firepower and armor plate to mobility.[79]

The M-26 medium tank

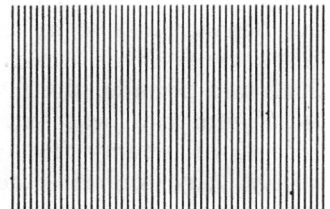

With the cessation of hostilities in Europe, a Theater General Board composed of senior field artillery officers convened to evaluate the contributions of the tank destroyer to the war effort. They based their study in part upon the after-action reports of forty-nine tank destroyer battalions that had fought in Europe. In its report, the board noted that the tank destroyer was "a most versatile weapon on the battlefield" and admitted that there existed a need for self-propelled, high-velocity guns within the infantry division, a function that the tank destroyers had fullfilled admirably.[80] The battalions sampled had destroyed, on the average, 34 German tanks and self-propelled guns, 17 artillery and antitank guns, and 16 pillboxes apiece, with one battalion claiming 105 tanks destroyed.[81] However, the board recognized the fact that tank destroyers had never validated the tank destroyer doctrine and, in fact, had not adhered to it on the battlefield.[82] The Theater General Board closed its report by recommending that high-velocity self-propelled guns be made organic to the infantry division, that Field Artillery assume responsibility for antitank defense-in-depth, that the Armored Force modify and adopt certain aspects of tank destroyer doctrine, and that "the tank destroyers as a separate force be discontinued."[83]

The report of the Theater General Board corresponded with the sentiments of General Jacob L. Devers, who became the commanding general of AGF in June 1945. Devers had never been a proponent of the tank destroyer concept. As head of the Armored Force in 1941, he had responded to the antitank victories in the GHQ maneuvers with the remark, "We were licked by a set of umpire rules."[84] The report he filed following his 1943 tour of Tunisia stated that the "tank destroyer arm is not a practical concept on the battlefield."[85] It came as no surprise that Devers simply allowed the tank destroyer program to expire in the great demobilization that followed World War II.

On 10 November 1945, the Tank Destroyer Center terminated its few remaining activities and, without fanfare, ceased to exist.[86] Officers commissioned in the tank destroyers found themselves transferred to the infantry. The mass inactivation of tank destroyer battalions began in the fall of 1945 and continued into the winter and spring of 1946. The very last tank destroyer battalion, the 656th, was inactivated at Camp Campbell, Kentucky, on 1 November 1946.[87] Although many of these battalions were later reactivated as tank formations, thus perpetuating the lineage of proud fighting units,[88] the tank destroyers were no more.

Conclusion

The tank destroyer concept, initiated by George C. Marshall, nurtured by Lesley J. McNair, and implemented by Andrew D. Bruce, was the U.S. Army's response to the revolution in warfare known as the blitzkrieg. It prescribed massed antitank elements, high-mobility units and vehicles, and high-velocity gunfire as the antidotes that would defeat massed tanks. The historian of the Tank Destroyer Center, writing in 1945, claimed that "tank destroyer doctrine as conceived and developed by Tank Destroyer Center in 1942 was so basically right in its vision and prescience that it stood all tests of combat missions."[1] However, as the foregoing chapters have demonstrated, the tank destroyer concept was never fully realized in combat, and, in fact, the successes attained by tank destroyer units in battle came about despite tank destroyer doctrine, not because of it.

In truth, tank destroyer doctrine was a fundamentally flawed set of principles. Today, the U.S. Army utilizes a methodical process for the development of new programs known as the Concept Based Requirements System (CBRS). Although no such process existed in 1942, by using CBRS as a model, one can identify the inconsistencies that attended the development of the tank destroyer concept.

In simplified form, CBRS consists of three major developmental stages. In the first stage, the Army identifies its mission and the opposition that the enemy can be expected to offer, with full consideration being given to past experience and to technological advances plotted for the future. Stage two involves translating that Army mission into specific battlefield and service functions to be performed by the various branches. The third stage consists of the simultaneous and integrated development of the doctrines, force structures, equipment, and training programs necessary for executing the battlefield functions that will fulfill the Army's mission. Thus, CBRS ensures that the Army's doctrines are attuned to the mission, the threat, and to each other.[2] By contrast, the development of the tank destroyer concept resulted in a product that was inapplicable to the battlefield and was poorly synchronized with the other arms.

In terms of the CBRS model, the tank destroyer's defects originated in stage one, with the identification of mission, threat, and technological trends. The U.S. Army's mission in World War II was overwhelmingly offensive in nature, but the very existence of a major antitank program implied a war in which the enemy held the initiative. Logically, this suggested that if the Army successfully pursued its mission, the tank destroyers would have little to do, and if the tank destroyers were fully engaged, the Army as a whole would be failing in its mission. In addition, the enemy threat was viewed primarily in terms of the blitzkrieg, even though the Germans would be on the strategic defensive by the time American troops encountered them in force. Tactically, the formulators of the tank destroyer concept acted on the assumption that the enemy fought in all-tank masses. As has been shown, German panzer doctrine actually encompassed all arms. Moreover, only 10 percent of the German Army was ever mechanized. Another fundamental lapse occurred in the realm of technological forecasting. Due in part to the lack of a central research and development agency, the Army completely failed to anticipate the advances in tank armor and armament that would occur as the war continued.

Given the misconceptions relating to the identification of mission, threat, and technological trends that occurred as part of the evolution of the tank destroyer, it follows logically that the development of battlefield functions would be flawed. Owing to the branch rivalries and obstructionism within the Army, antitank functions were not integrated into the activities of the existing arms but were instead assigned to the domain of a new tank destroyer quasi-arm. This encouraged the older arms to ignore the possibility that they might play a role in antitank combat. Inasmuch as the armored threat had been identified solely in terms of massed tanks, the new tank destroyer arm defined its battlefield function simply as that of stopping the tank—a rather narrow, technical task. The defeat of combined arms mechanized forces, which is a different matter altogether, was never perceived to be a tank destroyer function.

According to the CBRS paradigm, the final stages in developing the tank destroyer concept should have been the coordinated, simultaneous manifestation of force structures, equipment, and doctrine. In the case of tank destroyer development, however, the press of time and the bureaucratic nature of the Army fragmented these efforts among several agencies, but once undertaken, the tasks were at least addressed quickly. But due to the erroneous assumptions already built into the overarching tank destroyer concept, force structuring, doctrine formulation, and weapons development could not help but go astray.

The first task accomplished was the creation of a force structure. The tank destroyer battalion was essentially a single-arm antitank organization. Some tank destroyer advocates have suggested that the tank destroyer battalion was actually a precedent-setting combined arms team, but this was not the case. The tank destroyer battalion possessed the equivalent of only one infantry company (distributed among nine security sections) to support three tank destroyer companies, and it controlled no general purpose artillery. By contrast, the 1943 armored division, which was, indeed, a balanced, combined arms force, had the resources to pair up an infantry company and a howitzer battery to each tank company. The tank destroyer battalion was a single-arm force by intent because the assumption had already been made that the tank destroyer's function was a narrow one—the destruction of unsupported tanks.

The same assumption shaped the writing of doctrine. FM 18—5 (1942) exhorted the single-arm tank destroyer elements to defeat the single-arm threat through "offensive action" and "semi-independent" operations. The formula for potential tragedy was thus laid, for the real enemy was a master of combined arms warfare, not a single-arm threat. Experience in battle quickly showed that tank destroyers were, in reality, highly dependent on other arms for support, and that "offensive action" for them was often suicidal. The Tank Destroyer Center learned of these battlefield findings through the reports of AGF observers[3] and incorporated the lessons of combat in the 1944 edition of FM 18—5. This edition emphasized cooperation with other arms and made it clear that tank destroyer action was essentially defensive in nature. However, the gap between experience and doctrine never completely closed. FM 18—5 (1944) perpetuated the notion of massed, mobile tank destroyers but at the same time advocated closer coordination with the other arms, a policy that implied some degree of dispersal. Predictably, commanders in the field rectified this contradiction by quietly abandoning the theory of massing tank destroyer forces.

Finally, the failure to forecast technological advances early in the development of the tank destroyer concept resulted ultimately in the equipping of tank destroyer units with inadequate weapons. Neither the Tank Destroyer Center, nor AGF, nor the Ordnance Department ever fully appreciated the necessity of designing weapons for the future, not the present. Tank destroyer weapons designed in 1942 were largely unchanged in 1944, despite the fact that the Germans engaged in a furious arms race with the Soviets during the same period. However, the inadequacy of equipment was not a fatal blow to the tank destroyer concept. Even the finest weaponry would not have compensated for the conceptual and doctrinal flaws deeply embodied in the tank destroyer program. As evidence, witness the fact that the advent of the well-armed M-36 did little to reverse the abandonment of tank destroyer doctrine in the field. On the other hand, U.S. tanks were even less well armed than the tank destroyers, but because the armored establishment possessed a sound doctrine by 1944, armored formations succeeded on the battlefield in spite of their equipment. The historical evidence does not show that the tank destroyers tried to implement their doctrine but failed for the lack of proper equipment. Rather, it is clear that tank destroyer doctrine was never really executed because it rested on false premises and thus had little application on the battlefield.

For all of the conceptual blunders and doctrinal inadequacies that plagued the tank destroyer effort, the basic idea of massing antitank elements to defeat enemy armor was not necessarily disproven in World War II and did not die out completely with the inactivation of the tank destroyer force. Although the postwar Army officially adopted the premise advanced by General Devers that the best antitank weapon was the tank itself,[4] tank destroyer advocates continued to insist that, doctrinally and psychologically,

German Jagd Panther
tank hunter

tanks and tank destroyers were not interchangeable.[5] Technological advances made in recent years hold out renewed promise for the revival of certain tank destroyer concepts. Antitank guided missiles might offer the sure-kill capability that a latter-day tank destroyer would require, and they would, in portable form, provide the infantry with a degree of antitank self-sufficiency that would permit the massing of tank destroyer elements. Another modern antitank system, the attack helicopter, combines the firepower of the guided missile with a degree of mobility that the World War II tank destroyer could never approximate. The attack helicopter companies and battalions found within the divisions and corps of today's Army are the closest doctrinal heirs to the World War II tank destroyer concept.

Variations on the tank destroyer theme have met with considerable success in a number of foreign armies. During and after World War II, both the Germans and the Soviets produced large numbers of turretless tank hunter-assault guns, based on existing tank designs, that combined the virtues of high firepower, effective armor, and ease of production. (These fighting vehicles are sometimes called "tank destroyers," but they differed greatly from the American tank destroyer both in design and in doctrine.) The German and Soviet tank hunters were no more mobile than the tanks they were derived from, but they could stand and fight it out with enemy tanks, something that American tank destroyers were not always able to do.

The incentive to revive the tank destroyer weapons system grows proportionally with the rising price of the main battle tank. There might well be a place on the battlefield for a self-propelled weapon that can perform many of the direct-fire missions that do not require the full sophistication of the main battle tank. In recent publications, Richard E. Simpkin has proposed replacing the expensive and vulnerable main battle tank with two smaller and less-expensive types, one being a general purpose fire-support tank and the other a tank destroyer.[6]

Under what conditions would a modern doctrine analogous to the World War II tank destroyer concept prove successful? Combat experience showed that a single-arm tank destroyer force was ineffective against a combined arms foe. In 1973, however, massed Egyptian antitank elements scored a stunning success in combat along the banks of the Suez Canal, primarily

Soviet SU 100 assault gun

because Israeli doctrine had strayed from the principles of combined arms, with the result that Israeli tanks faced the Egyptian antitank missiles without support.

In cases where the enemy is not so obliging as to send out unsupported tanks, the same effect must be produced by breaking up the enemy's combined arms team. As noted in an earlier chapter, this tenet was first recognized in World War I: "Tanks unaccompanied by infantry cannot achieve desired success; they must be supported by infantry, who alone can clear and hold ground gained."[7] Moreover, "If the tanks succeed in penetrating the line, the [friendly] infantry must hold out and concentrate all their efforts on stopping the advance of the enemy's infantry while the hostile tanks are dealt with by our artillery."[8] The World War II tank destroyers focused their efforts solely on stopping tanks, but current doctrine maintains that in antimechanized operations, the "first dictum is to destroy the *combined arms integrity of the enemy at all levels while keeping the combined-arms integrity of your force intact.*"[9] Thus, the first precondition for any revival of the tank destroyer concept is that tank destroyers must be closely integrated with the other arms. The tank destroyer veterans of World War II would urge that tank destroyer elements must be made organic to the division. A tank destroyer unit held at the corps or army echelon must be a combined arms force in its own right.

A second precondition would be the provision of the infantry with adequate organic antitank and direct-fire support weapons. Otherwise, it would once again prove difficult to withdraw tank destroyers from the line for the purpose of massing them against major tank attacks.

The tank destroyer must mount a weapon superior to that of the tanks it will face and should be armored about as well as a tank. For any armored fighting vehicle to be completely effective as an antitank weapon, it must be able to trade blows with the enemy. The German and Soviet experience shows that both a revolving turret and superior mobility can be sacrificed to gain firepower and armor protection.

Another precondition would be the ability to develop operational and tactical intelligence that will allow tank destroyer elements to be emplaced prior to the enemy's mechanized attack. The World War II tank destroyers learned that elements not on hand when the enemy attack commenced did not arrive in time to affect the tactical outcome.

Any tank destroyer revival must include doctrinal provisions for the use of tank destroyers in secondary roles when massed enemy armor is not a threat. The value of tank destroyers in secondary missions during World War II was beyond question. As weapons grow in sophistication and cost, it is increasingly unlikely that any army could afford to field large specialized antitank elements that can perform no other functions in battle.

Finally, the successful reintroduction of a tank destroyer arm would require that higher commanders understand and accept the capabilities and limitations of tank destroyer forces. The best means of ensuring the development of rapport between the tank destroyers and the higher commander would be to make the tank destroyer unit an organic part of the formation with which it will go to war. Above all, it must not be forgotten that successful armored operations are conducted by combined arms forces, and that any attempt to counter them must involve the employment of tank destroyers as one part of a combined arms team.

Even if the tank destroyer concept is never revived, the tank destroyers of World War II should not be forgotten, for they dealt telling blows to the armies of the Axis nations. On battlefields ranging from Tunisia to Luzon, tank destroyers were a highly valued asset, whether employed on direct-fire, indirect-fire, or antitank missions. The tank destroyer program also made a psychological contribution to the war effort by reducing the unreasonable fear of the tank that permeated all ranks and branches in the early days of the war. This victory of the mind was accomplished through a bold and convincing insistence that the tank, too, had its vulnerabilities. Even on the few occasions when technologically superior panzer forces assailed American arms in strength, the presence of tank destroyers helped curb the panic that had swept away earlier victims of the blitzkrieg.

When viewed in the context of the overall American war effort, the U.S. Army's tank destroyer program represented a reflexive response to the stark threat posed by mechanized warfare. Like the human body's reaction to sudden danger, the tank destroyer reflex was neither perfectly coordinated nor fully thought out. In many respects, it tended toward excess. However unmethodical and misguided the tank destroyer response may have been, in 1942 it was far preferable for the U.S. Army to overreact to the armored threat than to ignore the tank or to assume that it could not be defeated. The damage done to the American military effort by diverting tank destroyers to secondary missions and inactivating surplus battalions was minimal compared to that which might have been caused by the absence of any antitank program whatsoever. Seek, Strike, and Destroy ultimately failed as a doctrinal concept, but the tank destroyers themselves created success where it counted most—on the decisive battlefields of World War II.

Notes

Chapter 1

1. John Weeks, *Men Against Tanks, A History of Antitank Warfare* (New York: Mason/ Charter 1975), 22—25.

2. U.S. War Department, War Plans Division, "Instructions for Anti-tank Defence (Provisional— February 1918) from an Official British Document," War Department Document no. 783 (April 1918), 7.

3. Ibid., 9.

4. Ibid., 12.

5. Ibid., 9.

6. Quoted in Mary Stubbs and Stanley R. Connor, *Armor-Cavalry,* pt. 1, *Regular Army and Army Reserve,* Army Lineage Series (Washington, DC: Office of the Chief of Military History, U.S. Army, 1969), 50.

7. Weeks, *Men Against Tanks,* 31.

8. For an analysis of the panzer division, see Richard M. Ogorkiewicz, *Armoured Forces* (New York: Arco, 1970), 72—75. Kenneth Macksey, *Tank Pioneers* (New York: Arco, 1981) is a recent reinterpretation of armored development through World War II that sheds some fresh insight upon early tank developments.

9. Kent Roberts Greenfield, Robert R. Palmer, and Bell I. Wiley, *The Organization of Ground Combat Troops,* U.S. Army in World War II: The Army Ground Forces (Washington, DC: Historical Division, United States Army, 1947) 174—75. For details of the 1937 division tests, see L. Van L. Naisawald, "The U.S. Infantry Division, Changing Concepts in Organization 1900—1939" (Baltimore: Operations Research Office, Johns Hopkins University, 1952).

10. U.S. Army Command and General Staff School, *Antitank Defense (Tentative)* (Fort Leavenworth KS, 1936), and U.S. Army Command and General Staff School, *Antimechanized Defense (Tentative)* (Fort Leavenworth, KS, 1939). See, for example, *Antimechanized Defense,* 14—15 for a summary of the proposed doctrine.

11. U.S. War Department, FM 100—5, *Tentative Field Service Regulations: Operations* (Washington, DC: U.S. Government Printing Office, 1939), 77.

12. Ibid., 77—78.

13. Weeks, *Men Against Tanks,* 30—34; Harry C. Thomson and Lida Mayo, *The Ordnance Department: Procurement and Supply,* U.S. Army in World War II The Technical Services (Washington, DC: Office of the Chief of Military History, Department of the Army, 1960), 80—84.

74

14. Weeks, *Men Against Tanks,* 96.

15. Greenfield, Palmer, and Wiley, *Organization,* 274—75.

16. FM 100—5 (1939), 6.

17. Alistair Horne, *To Lose a Battle, France 1940* (Boston: Little, Brown and Co., 1969), 182.

18. Robert A. Doughty, "French Antitank Doctrine 1940: The Antidote that Failed," *Military Review* 56 (May 1976):36—48.

19. Quoted in ibid., 36—37.

20. Ibid., 40.

21. Jean Dupont, "Fighting the Panzers," *Field Artillery Journal* 31 (August 1941):538—43.

22. Basil Henry Liddell Hart, *The German Generals Talk* (New York: W. Morrow, 1948), 94.

23. "Artillery and the Tank," *Field Artillery Journal* 30 (July—August 1940):243—48.

24. O. F. Marston, "Fast Moving Targets," *Field Artillery Journal* 30 (July—August 1940): 264—67.

25. Ralph Van Wyck, "Antitank Battery Training," *Field Artillery Journal* 30 (January 1941): 6—10.

26. Greenfield, Palmer, and Wiley, *Organization,* 274—75; "Newly Approved Organization, Divisional Artillery—Triangular Division," *Field Artillery Journal* 30 (September—October 1940): 336.

27. See Emory A. Dunham, "Tank Destroyer History," Army General Forces Study no. 29 (N.p.: Historical Section, Army Ground Forces, 1946), 1.

28. U.S. War Department, FM 100—5, *Field Service Regulations; Operations* (Washington, DC: U.S. Government Printing Office, 1941), 160.

29. Dunham, "Tank Destroyer History," 1.

30. Quoted in U.S. Army Tank Destroyer Center, "Tank Destroyer History" (Camp Hood, TX, 1945?), pt. 1, chap. 1,3. This document is available on microfilm from the Library of Congress.

31. Memo, Assistant Chief of Staff, G-3, to Chief of Staff, 19 April 1941, Subject: Creation of Additional Antitank-Antiaircraft Units, Andrew D. Bruce Papers, U.S. Army Military History Institute, Carlisle Barracks, PA (hereafter cited as MHI).

32. Memo, Chief of Staff to Assistant Chief of Staff, G-3, 14 May 1941, Subject: Defense Against Armored Forces, George C. Marshall Papers, George C. Marshall Research Library, Lexington, VA (hereafter cited as Marshall Library).

33. Tank Destroyer Center, "History," pt. 1, chap. 1, 7—8.

34. Untitled document, item 4327, microfilm reel 287, Marshall Library.

35. A. C. Wedemeyer, "Antitank Defense," *Field Artillery Journal* 31 (May 1941):258—72. Wedemeyer's article also appears as "Stopping the Armored Onslaught," *Infantry Journal* 48 (May 1941):22—31.

36. Quoted in Tank Destroyer Center, "History," pt. 1, chap. 1, 3—4.

37. Tank Destroyer Center, "History," pt. 1, chap. 1, 5, 7—8.

38. For a discussion of streamlining and pooling, see Greenfield, Palmer, and Wiley, *Organization,* 276—80.

39. Adjutant General, GHQ, to Commanding General, Third Army, 8 August 1941, Subject: GHQ Antitank Units in GHQ Directed Maneuvers, 353 Training Directives, GHQ, entry

57, Record Group 337, National Archives, Washington, DC (hereafter cited as NA); U.S. Army, GHQ Provisional Antitank Groups, Performance of Antitank, entry 57D, Record Group 337, NA.

40. Comments by Lt. Gen. L. J. McNair, 1st Phase, GHQ-Directed Maneuvers, Camp Polk, Louisiana, 14—19 September 1941, Bruce Papers, MHI. For an operational analysis of the 1941 maneuvers, see Christopher R. Gabel, "The U.S. Army GHQ Maneuvers of 1941" (Ph.D. dissertation, Ohio State University, 1981; microfilm, Ann Arbor, MI: University Microfilms International, 1981).

41. See Gabel, "GHQ Maneuvers," 83—85, 206—13.

42. Maneuvers Memo No. 49, HQ First Army, 31 October 1941, Subject: Special Task Forces, First Army Maneuvers 1941 Final Report, entry 57D, Record Group 337, NA.

43. Gabel, "GHQ Maneuvers," 243—49.

44. Matters to be covered in critique, Maj. B. P. Purdue, Performance of Antitank, entry 57D, Record Group 337, NA.

45. Second Phase 1 and 2 Armored Divisions, entry 57D, Record Group 337, NA.

46. Maj. Gen. Jacob Devers, quoted in "Second Battle of the Carolinas," *Time*, 8 December 1941:66.

47. Memo for the Secretary [of War], Notes on Conference, 4 December 1941, item 2714, microfilm reel 116, Marshall Library.

48. Tank Destroyer Center, "History," pt. 1, chap. 1, 15.

49. Conference in the Office of the Chief of Staff, 7 October 1941, item 4327, microfilm reel 287, Marshall Library.

50. Tank Destroyer Center, "History," pt. 1, chap. 1, 16.

51. Ibid., pt. 1, chap. 2, annex A; and pt. 1, chap. 1, 17.

52. Ibid., pt. 1, chap. 1, 16.

Chapter 2

1. See Greenfield, Palmer, and Wiley, *Organization*, for a thorough treatment of AGF's role and activities.

2. Quoted in Greenfield, Palmer, and Wiley, *Organization*, 389.

3. Quoted in Tank Destroyer Center, "History," pt. 1, chap. 1, 13.

4. Dunham, "Tank Destroyer History," 9.

5. Memo, Col. A. D. Bruce for the Assistant Chief of Staff, G-3, 21 January 1942, Subject: Report on the Maneuver Experiences of Provisional Antitank Battalions (First Army), item 4327, microfilm reel 287, Marshall Library.

6. Tank Destroyer Center, "History," pt. 1, chap. 2, 16.

7. "New Tank Destroyer Battalions," *Infantry Journal* 50 (January 1942):56—59.

8. Tank Destroyer Center, "History," pt. 1, chap. 6, 30.

9. Robert W. Green, to the author, 22 May 1977. Green was a first lieutenant at the Tank Destroyer Center during World War II.

10. Tank Destroyer Center, "History," pt. 1, chap. 1, 4.

11. Memo, Chief of Staff to Assistant Chief of Staff, G-3, 14 May 1941, Subject: Defense Against Armored Forces, Marshall Papers, Marshall Library.

12. Quoted in Tank Destroyer Center, "History," pt. 1, chap. 1, 13.

13. Adjutant General, GHQ, to Commanding General, Third Army, 8 August 1941, Subject: GHQ Antitank Units in GHQ Directed Maneuvers, 353 Training Objectives, GHQ, entry 57, Record Group 337, NA.

14. Maneuvers Memo No. 49, 31 October 1941, First Army Maneuvers 1941, First Report, entry 57D, Record Group 337, NA.

15. Provisional Tank Destroyer Battalion GHQ, "Standing Operating Procedure" (Fort George G. Meade, MD, 1941), item 4327, microfilm reel 287, Marshall Library; Tank Destroyer Center, "History," pt. 1, chap. 2, 12; Dunham, "Tank Destroyer History," 21.

16. Tank Destroyer Center, "History," pt. 1, chap. 2, 12—14; and pt. 1, chap. 8, 1.

17. Ibid., pt. 1, chap. 1, 13.

18. Conference in the Office of the Chief of Staff, 7 October 1941, item 4327, microfilm reel 287, Marshall Library.

19. U.S. War Department, FM 18—5, *Tank Destroyer Field Manual, Organization and Tactics of Tank Destroyer Units* (Washington, DC: U.S. Government Printing Office, 1942), iv.

20. Ibid., 3—5.

21. Ibid., 2, 5.

22. Ibid., 19.

23. Ibid., 7.

24. Ibid., 22, 69.

25. Ibid., 52.

26. Ibid., 20—23, 53—54.

27. Ibid., 20—21, 29—30, 32.

28. Ibid., 28.

29. Ibid., 7.

30. Ibid., 19—20.

31. Ibid., 188.

32. Ibid., 14.

33. Ibid., 8.

34. Ibid., 23, 94.

35. Ibid., 23.

36. Charles M. Baily, *Faint Praise: American Tanks and Tank Destroyers During World War II* (Hamden, CT: Archon, 1983), 21—22.

37. Ibid.

38. Tank Destroyer Center, "History," pt. 1, chap. 6, 15.

39. Baily, *Faint Praise,* 27, 31; Brig. Gen. W. B. Palmer to Maj. Gen. A. D. Bruce, 9 December 1942, Bruce Papers, MHI.

40. Peter Chamberlain and Chris Ellis, *British and American Tanks of World War II* (New York: Arco, 1981), 147—48. A comparable medium tank, the M-4 Sherman, had a top speed of about twenty-five miles per hour and weighed approximately thirty-three tons. Chamberlain and Ellis, *Tanks,* 115.

41. Maj. Gen. Andrew D. Bruce to Commanding Officer, 307th Infantry, 10 May 1945, Bruce Papers, MHI.

42. See Baily, *Faint Praise,* 48—50, and 67—68, for the evolution of the M-18.

43. Tank Destroyer Center, "History," pt. 1, chap. 1, 12; pt. 1, chap. 2, 8—9; Baily, *Faint Praise,* 39.

44. See Baily, *Faint Praise,* 39—47, for a thorough discussion of the expedient weapons.

45. Maj. Gen. A. D. Bruce to Brig. Gen. W. B. Palmer, 26 January 1943, Bruce Papers, MHI; Baily, *Faint Praise,* 45—47.

46. Dunham, "Tank Destroyer History," 11.

47. For a detailed chronology of tank destroyer activities at Camp Hood, see Tank Destroyer Center, "History," and a derivative study, Dunham, "Tank Destroyer History."

48. FM 18—5 (1942), iv.

49. Ibid., 128.

50. Ibid., 123—26.

51. Tank Destroyer Center, "History," pt. 1, chap. 8, 25—28.

52. Ibid., pt. 1, chap. 2, 20; and pt. 1, chap. 3, 22.

53. Maj. Gen. A. D. Bruce to "Westy" [Col. Wendell Westover?], 6 March 1945, Bruce Papers, MHI.

54. Green, to author, 22 May 1977.

55. A total of four battalions in the North African campaign used the M-3. Shelby L. Stanton, *Order of Battle: U.S. Army World War II* (Novato, CA: Presidio Press, 1984), 333—38.

56. Dunham, "Tank Destroyer History," 26.

Chapter 3

1. Maj. Allerton Cushman, [Army Ground Forces] Observer Report, 29 March 1943, 2—3, Documents Collection, Combined Arms Research Library, U.S. Army Command and General Staff College, Fort Leavenworth, KS (hereafter cited as CARL).

2. Allied Forces G-3 Training Section, "Training Notes from Recent Fighting in Tunisia: Experiences, Observations, and Opinions Collected from Officers and Men of Front Line Units, March 18—30, 1943," 62—63, CARL.

3. Ibid., 63.

4. "Provisional Instructions for Leadership and Action of the Tank Regiment and Tank Battalion," 13, 17, captured German document translated by Great Britain, Army, General Headquarters, Middle East, GSI, Box 56, [19]21—41, Armored Tactics, Patton Collection, Library of Congress. See also Great Britain, War Office, General Staff, "German Armoured Tactics in Libya," Periodical Notes on the German Army no. 37, February 1942, CARL.

5. Baily, *Faint Praise,* 152—55, offers technical data of tank destroyer weapons.

6. Cushman, [Army Ground Forces] Observer Report, 3 May 1943, CARL, 6.

7. FM 18—5 (1942), 14.

8. Allied Forces, "Training Notes," 23—24.

9. Cushman, Observer Report, 29 March 1943, 5.

10. Allied Forces, "Training Notes," 26.

11. See Baily, *Faint Praise,* 154, for technical data.

12. Gilbert A. Ellman, "Panther vs. Panzer," *Military Review* 24 (August 1944):21—26.

13. Ibid.

14. U.S. Army Tank Destroyer School, "Tank Destroyer Combat," Camp Hood, TX, n.d., Bruce Papers, MHI, 16.

15. Ibid.

16. For details on the German attack at Sidi-bou-Zid, see George F. Howe, *Northwest Africa: Seizing the Initiative in the West,* U.S. Army in World War II: The Mediterranean Theater of Operations (Washington, DC: Office of the Chief of Military History, Department of the Army, 1957), 410—15; and William R. Betson, "Sidi-Bou-Zid—A Case History of Failure," *Armor* 91 (November—December 1982):38—44.

17. Ibid.

18. Howe, *Northwest Africa,* 430—35; Cushman, Observer Report, 3 May 1943, 2; Cushman, Observer Report, 29 March 1943, 4.

19. Howe, *Northwest Africa,* 460—64.

20. Howe, *Northwest Africa,* 559—60; Tank Destroyer School, "Tank Destroyer Combat," 17—30; Cushman, Observer Report, 3 May 1943, 1.

21. U.S. Army Ground Forces Board, North African Theater of Operations, Report A-165, 20 June 1944, CARL; U.S. Army Ground Forces Board, Mediterranean Theater of Operations, "Tank Destroyer Conference, Florence, Italy," November 1944, CARL, 8.

22. U.S. Army Ground Forces Board, Mediterranean Theater of Operations, "The Tank Destroyer Battalion in Action," Report A, Misc-21, 24 May 1944, 4—5, CARL.

23. Ibid., 4.

24. AGF Board Report A-165.

25. AGF Board MTO, "Tank Destroyer Conference," 3.

26. Green, to the author, 22 May 1977.

27. E. N. Harmon, "Notes on Combat Experience During the Tunisian and African Campaigns," 11, typescript, Library, U.S. Army Armor School, Fort Knox, KY.

28. AGF Board MTO, "Tank Destroyer Conference," 6.

29. Ibid.

30. Allied Forces, "Training Notes," 71.

31. FM 18—5 (1942), 109.

32. Harmon, "Notes," 9.

33. AGF Board MTO, "Tank Destroyer Battalion," 7—8; AGF Board MTO, "Tank Destroyer Conference," 8.

34. Ibid.

35. U.S. Army, 5th Army, Training Memo no. 60, "Employment of Tank Destroyer Units as Reinforcing Artillery," 24 August 1943, CARL; P. C. Meachem, "A New Fighting Team," *Field Artillery Journal* 34 (November 1944):778—80.

36. AGF Board MTO, "Tank Destroyer Battalion," 7—8.

37. Ibid., 5—9.

38. Training Memo no. 60.

39. AGF Board Report A-165.

40. Ibid.

41. AGF Board MTO, "Tank Destroyer Conference," 7.

42. AGF Board MTO, "Tank Destroyer Battalion," 6—7.

43. AGF Board MTO, "Tank Destroyer Conference," 6—7.

44. Ibid.

45. Bruce to "Westy," 6 March 1945.

46. Tank Destroyer Center, "History," pt. 1, chap. 8, 15—16.

47. FM 18—5 (1942), 19.

48. Maj. Gen. A. D. Bruce to Lt. Gen. Lesley J. McNair, 5 June 1943, Bruce Papers, MHI; AGF Board MTO, "Tank Destroyer Battalion," 6.

49. Allied Forces Training Memorandum no. 23, "Employment of Tank Destroyer Units," 21 March 1943, CARL.

50. Cushman, Observer Report, 3 May 1943, 1.

51. Ibid., 20.

52. Ibid., 21.

53. Ibid., 1, 21.

54. Maj. Gen. J. P. Lucas, Extract from Report on Sicilian Campaign, 8 September 1943, Bruce Papers, MHI.

55. Greenfield, Palmer, and Wiley, *Organization*, 425, 427.

56. Harmon, "Notes," 13.

57. Extract of General Devers' Report, 9 February 1943, Bruce Papers, MHI.

58. George C. Marshall, Chief of Staff, to Maj. Gen. A. D. Bruce, 30 January 1943, Bruce Papers, MHI.

59. Lt. Col. George M. Dean to Maj. Gen. A. D. Bruce, 19 June 1943, Bruce Papers, MHI.

60. Brig. Gen. B. M. Sawbridge to Maj. Gen. A. D. Bruce, 19 March 1943, Bruce Papers, MHI.

61. Greenfield, Palmer, and Wiley, *Organization*, 414.

62. Tank Destroyer Center, "History," pt. 1, chap. 3, 21.

63. Ibid., pt. 1, chap. 1, 15.

64. Greenfield, Palmer, and Wiley, *Organization*, 161.

65. Stanton, *Order of Battle*, 333—38.

66. Memo, G-3 War Department General Staff for the Chief of Staff, 20 January 1944, quoted in Greenfield, Palmer, and Wiley, *Organization*, 237.

67. Stanton, *Order of Battle*, 333—38.

68. Tank Destroyer Center, "History," pt. 1, chap. 4, 21.

69. Cushman, Observer Report, 3 May 1943, 2.

70. U.S. Army, Armored School, "The Employment of Four Tank Destroyer Battalions in the ETO," student research report by Committee 24 (Fort Knox, KY, May 1950), Figure 1; U.S. Army Command and General Staff School, FM 101—10 (Tentative), *Staff Officer's*

Field Manual: Organization, Technical, and Logistical Data (Fort Leavenworth, KS, 1943), para. 126.

71. Greenfield, Palmer, and Wiley, *Organization*, 402, 430; Dunham, "Tank Destroyer History," 333—35.

72. Tank Destroyer Center, "History," pt. 3, chap. 1, 14—15, and pt. 2, chap. 1, 5—6.

73. Greenfield, Palmer, and Wiley, *Organization*, 426—27.

74. Ibid; Speech by General A. D. Bruce on Field Manual 18—5, Hood Road Theater, 21 May 1943, Bruce Papers, MHI.

75. Maj. Gen A. D. Bruce to Lt. Col. James P. Barney, Jr., 1 May 1943, Bruce Papers, MHI.

76. Speech by General Bruce on FM 18—5, 21 May 1943.

77. Ibid.

78. FM 18—5 (1942), iv.

79. Dunham, "Tank Destroyer History," 27; Greenfield, Palmer, and Wiley, *Organization,* 427.

80. FM 101—10 (Tentative), [1943], para. 127—28.

81. Baily, *Faint Praise,* 65—66.

82. Tank Destroyer Center, "History," pt. 1, chap. 8, 16.

83. AGF Board MTO, "Tank Destroyer Conference," 4.

Chapter 4

1. FM 18—20, FM 18—21, FM 18—22, and FM 18—23, respectively.

2. U.S. War Department, FM 18—5, *Tactical Employment Tank Destroyer Unit* (Washington, DC: U.S. Government Printing Office, 1944), 5.

3. Ibid.

4. Ibid.

5. U.S. War Department, FM 18—20, *Tactical Employment of Tank Destroyer Platoon Self-Propelled* (Washington, DC: U.S. Government Printing Office, 1944), 26.

6. FM 18—5 (1942), 32.

7. Lt. Gen. Lesley J. McNair to Maj. Gen. Orlando Ward, 2 August 1943, Orlando Ward Papers, MHI.

8. FM 18—5 (1944), 51—52, 55—56.

9. Ibid., 5.

10. Ibid., 52—53, 76.

11. Ibid., 52.

12. Ibid., 3.

13. Ibid., 65.

14. Ibid., 6.

15. Ibid., 65.

16. Ibid., 4, 81.

17. Ibid., 79, 84—85, 87, 89.

18. U.S. Forces, European Theater, General Board, "Report on Study of Organization, Equipment, and Tactical Employment of Tank Destroyer Units" [1946?], 2 (hereafter cited as USFET, General Board, "Tank Destroyer Units").

19. See U.S. War Department, FM 7—35, *Antitank Company, Infantry Regiment and Antitank Platoon, Infantry Battalion* (Washington, DC: U.S. Government Printing Office, 1944).

20. FM 18—5 (1944), 3.

21. Ibid., 3—4, 6—8.

22. Cushman, Observer Report, 3 May 1943, 15.

23. Matthew Cooper, *The German Army, 1933—1945* (New York: Bonanza, 1984), 496—97; Carlo D'Este, *Decision in Normandy* (New York: E. P. Dutton, 1983), 74—75; Nigel Hamilton, *Master of the Battlefield: Monty's War Years 1942—44* (New York: McGraw-Hill, 1983), 583.

24. USFET, General Board, "Tank Destroyer Units," 2.

25. Stanton, *Order of Battle*, 326—38.

26. U.S. Army Field Forces, "Type Field Army," 1 July 1949, para. 504, CARL.

27. Baily, *Faint Praise*, 90.

28. USFET, General Board, "Tank Destroyer Units," 2.

29. Baily, *Faint Praise*, 2—3.

30. Ibid., 90.

31. Ibid., 106.

32. U.S. Army, 1st Army, "Artillery Information Service," September 1944, 61.

33. Baily, *Faint Praise*, 70—74.

34. USFET, General Board, "Tank Destroyer Units," 2.

35. U. S. Army, 1st Army, "Artillery Information Service," December 1944, 82.

36. U.S. Army, 814th Tank Destroyer Battalion, After-Action Report, December 1944, CARL.

37. First U.S. Army, "Artillery Information Service," December 1944, 63.

38. Ibid., 82.

39. U.S. Army Ground Forces, Immediate Report no. 63, HQ, 12th Army Group 24 September 1944, comments of Col. L. E. Jacoby; 1st Army, "Artillery Information Service," December 1944, 64.

40. Great Britain, War Office, *Notes From Theatres of War, no. 20* Italy 1943/1944 (N.p., 1945), 39; Great Britain, Army, 21st Army Group, "Extracts of 21st Army Group AFV Technical Report 26," 22 May 1945.

41. Col. C. R. Landon to Commanding General, European Theater of Operations, U.S. Army, 9 November 1944, Bruce Papers, MHI.

42. Stanton, *Order of Battle*, 47—69, 75—188, 299—302.

43. First U.S. Army, "Artillery Information Service," December 1944, 39—90.

44. Capt. Frederick H. Parkin, "The Employment of the Tank Destroyer Battalion with the Infantry Division," 12 March 1945, CARL.

45. Ibid.

46. John Lemp and Ernest C. Hatfield, "Tank Destroyers as Assault Guns," *Field Artillery Journal* 35 (April 1945):244—45.

47. First U.S. Army, "Artillery Information Service," September 1944, 57.

48. U.S. Army Ground Forces, Immediate Report no. 58, 16—17 September 1944. See also 1st Army, "Artillery Information Service," July 1944, 61.

49. First U.S. Army, "Artillery Information Service," December 1944, 62.

50. USFET, General Board, "Tank Destroyer Units," 23—24; U.S. Army Ground Forces Report no. 20 309, 25 November 1944, CARL.

51. Paul B. Bell, "Tank Destroyers in the Roer River Crossing," *Field Artillery Journal* 35 (August 1945):497—98.

52. First U.S. Army, "Artillery Information Service," September 1944, 57—58.

53. U.S. Army Ground Forces, Immediate Report no. 6, European Theater of Operations, 3 February 1945, CARL.

54. U.S. Army Ground Forces, Immediate Report 88, European Theater of Operations, 12th Army Group, 30 October 1944, CARL.

55. Eugene T. Oborn, "Proper Use and Abuse of Tank Destroyers," *Field Artillery Journal* 35 (July 1945):398—99.

56. U.S. Army, 1st Army, Operations Memo no. 37, 9 July 1944, Subject: Employment of Tank Destroyers, found in U.S. Army Ground Forces Board Report no. C-100, European Theater of Operations, 25 August 1944, CARL.

57. USFET, General Board, "Tank Destroyer Units," 14—15.

58. Ibid., 14—16.

59. Stanton, *Order of Battle*, 328—31; USFET, General Board, "Tank Destroyer Units," 6.

60. U.S. Army, 3d Army, After-Action Report, pt. 24, Tank Destroyers, April 1945, CARL.

61. U.S. Army Ground Forces, Immediate Report no. 88, European Theater of Operations, 12th Army Group, 30 October 1944, comments Lt. Col. H. L. Davisson, Commanding Officer, 634th Tank Destroyer Battalion, CARL.

62. U.S. Army Ground Forces Board, Report no. C-190, European Theater of Operations, 25 August 1944, CARL.

63. Parkin, "Tank Destroyer Battalion."

64. For the Mortain battle see: Martin Blumenson, *Breakout and Pursuit*, U.S. Army in World War II: The European Theater of Operations (1961; reprint, Washington, DC: Office of the Chief of Military History, U.S. Army, 1970), 461; Armored School, "Employment," 81—111; First Army, "Artillery Information Service," September 1944, 59—60 and December 1944, 72; USFET, General Board, "Tank Destroyer Units," 15.

65. For the Arracourt battle see: Armored School, "Employment," 64—80; Hugh M. Cole, *The Lorraine Campaign*, U.S. Army in World War II: The European Theater of Operations (1950; reprint, Washington, DC: Historical Division, U.S. Army, 1981), 222—25.

66. Hugh M. Cole, *The Ardennes: Battle of the Bulge*, U.S. Army in World War II: The European Theater of Operations (1965; reprint, Washington, DC: Office of the Chief of Military History, U.S. Army, 1983), 147, 281.

67. Ibid., 199, 323—24.

68. Ibid., 126; Armored School, "Employment," 58; 1st U.S. Army, "Artillery Information Service," May 1945, 94.

69. Robert W. Hasbrouck, interview with Gregory Fontenot, Washington, DC, 20 August 1984; Bruce C. Clarke, interview with Gregory Fontenot, McLean, VA, 19 August 1984.

70. Cole, *Ardennes*, 308—9, 453, 472—74.

71. First U.S. Army, "Artillery Information Service," May 1945, 81; 3d Army, After-Action Report, pt. 24, 3.

72. First U.S. Army, "Artillery Information Service," May 1945, 81.

73. USFET, General Board, "Tank Destroyer Units," 2.

74. Baily, *Faint Praise*, 115.

75. D. L. McCaskey, "The Role of Army Ground Forces in the Development of Equipment," Army Ground Forces Study no. 29 (N.p.: Historical Section, Army Ground Forces, 1946), 66—67.

76. Stanton, *Order of Battle*, 333—38; R. L. McNelly, "Tank Destroyers at Work—Without the Book," *Field Artillery Journal* 35 (July 1945):396—98.

77. Dunham, "Tank Destroyer History," 45.

78. Allerton Cushman, "Tank Destroyers Against Japan," *Field Artillery Journal* 36 (February 1946):70—73.

79. Chamblerlain and Ellis, *Tanks,* 158. See Baily, *Faint Praise*, for an analysis of the development and procurement of the M-26.

80. USFET, General Board, "Tank Destroyer Units," 10, 29.

81. Ibid., 25.

82. Ibid., 10.

83. Ibid., 29.

84. "Second Battle of the Carolinas," *Time*, 8 December 1941:66.

85. Extract of General Devers' Report, 9 February 1943, Bruce Papers, MHI.

86. Stanton, *Order of Battle,* 26.

87. Ibid., 333—38.

88. See James A. Sawicki, *Tank Battalions of the U.S. Army* (Dumfries, VA: Wyvern, 1983).

Chapter 5

1. Tank Destroyer Center, "History," pt. 4, chap. 1, 4—5.

2. U.S. Army Training and Doctrine Command, Regulation no. 11—7, *Operational Concepts and Army Doctrine*, (Fort Monroe, VA, 1982).

3. Copies of nearly every wartime observer report cited in this study are known to have been sent to the Tank Destroyer Center.

4. Robert A. Doughty, *The Evolution of U.S. Army Doctrine, 1946—76*, Leavenworth Paper no. 1 (Fort Leavenworth, KS: Combat Studies Institute, U.S. Army Command and General Staff College, 1979), 4.

5. G. D. W. Court, *Hard Pounding* (Washington, DC: The U.S. Field Artillery Association, 1946), 6—7.

6. Richard E. Simpkin, *Antitank: An Airmechanized Response to Armored Threats in the 90s* (New York: Brassey's, 1982), 176—77, 186.

7. U.S. War Department, "Instructions for Anti-tank Defence," 9.

8. Ibid.

9. U.S. Army Infantry School, TC 7—24, *Antiarmor Techniques for Mechanized Infantry* (Fort Benning, GA, 1975), pt. 2, 2.

Bibliography

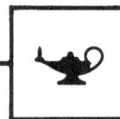

Abbreviations

CARL—Documents Collection, Combined Arms Research Library, U.S. Army Command and General Staff College, Fort Leavenworth. KS.

MHI—U.S. Army Military History Institute, Carlisle Barracks, PA.

NA—National Archives, Washington, DC.

Documents

Unpublished

Allied Forces. Training Memorandum no. 23. "Employment of Tank Destroyer Units." 21 March 1943. CARL.

Allied Forces. G-3 Training Section. "Training Notes from Recent Fighting in Tunisia: Experiences, Observations, and Opinions Collected from Officers and Men of Front Line Units, March 18—30, 1943." CARL.

Bruce, Andrew D. Papers. U.S. Army Military History Institute, Carlisle Barracks, PA.

Conference in the Office of the Chief of Staff, 7 October 1941. Item 4327, microfilm reel 287, George C. Marshall Research Library, Lexington, VA.

Cushman, Allerton, Maj. [Army Ground Forces] Observer Report. 29 March 1943. CARL.

Dunham, Emory A. "Tank Destroyer History." Army Ground Forces Study no. 29. N.p.: Historical Section, Army Ground Forces, 1946. CARL.

Entry 57, General HQ, U.S. Army (GHQ). Record Group 337 (HQ Army Ground Forces). NA.

Entry 57D, General HQ, U.S. Army (GHQ). General Staff, G-3 Section, Subject File: 1940—March 9, 1942. Record Group 337 (HQ Army Ground Forces). NA.

Great Britain, Army. 21st Army Group. "Extracts of 21 Army Group AFV Technical Report 26." 22 May 1943. CARL.

Great Britain. War Office. General Staff. "German Armoured Tactics in Libya." Periodical Notes on the German Army no. 37. February 1942. CARL.

Harmon, E. N. "Notes on Combat Experience During the Tunisian and African Campaigns." Typescript, Library, U.S. Army Armor School, Fort Knox, KY.

McCaskey, D. L. "The Role of Army Ground Forces in the Development of Equipment." Army Ground Forces Study no. 34. N.p.: Historical Section, Army Ground Forces, 1946. CARL.

Marshall, George C. Papers. George C. Marshall Research Library, Lexington, VA.

Memo, Col. A. D. Bruce for the Assistant Chief of Staff, G-3, 21 January 1942, Subject: Report on the Maneuver Experiences of Provisional Antitank Battalions (First Army). Item 4327, microfilm reel 287, George C. Marshall Library, Lexington, VA.

Memo for the Secretary [of War], Notes on Conference, 4 December 1941. Item 2714, microfilm reel 116, George C. Marshall Library, Lexington, VA.

Naisawald, L. Van L. "The U.S. Infantry Division, Changing Concepts in Organization, 1900—1939." Baltimore: Operations Research Office, Johns Hopkins University, 1952. CARL.

Parkin, Frederick H., Capt. "The Employment of the Tank Destroyer Battalion with the Infantry Division." 12 March 1945. CARL.

"Provisional Instructions for Leadership and Action of the Tank Regiment and Tank Battalion." Captured German document translated by Great Britain, Army, General Headquarters, Middle East, CSI. Box 56, Armored Tactics, Patton Collection, Library of Congress.

Provisional Tank Destroyer Battalion GHQ. "Standing Operating Procedure." Fort George G. Meade, MD, 1941? Item 4327, Microfilm reel 287, George C. Marshall Research Library, Lexington, VA.

U.S. Army. Armored School. "The Employment of Four Tank Destroyer Battalions in the ETO." Student research report by Committee 24. Fort Knox, KY, May 1950. CARL.

U.S. Army. 1st Army. "Artillery Information Service." CARL.

U.S. Army. 1st Army. Operations Memo no. 37. 9 July 1944. Subject: Employment of Tank Destroyers. In U.S. Army Ground Forces Board. Report no. C-100. European Theater of Operations. 25 August 1944. CARL.

U.S. Army. 3d Army. After-Action Report. Pt. 24. Tank Destroyers. April 1945. CARL.

U.S. Army. 5th Army. Training Memo no. 60. "Employment of Tank Destroyer Units as Reinforcing Artillery." 24 August 1943. CARL.

U.S. Army Field Forces. "Type Field Army." 1 July 1949. CARL.

U.S. Army Ground Forces. Immediate Report no. 6. European Theater of Operations. 3 February 1945. CARL.

U.S. Army Ground Forces. Immediate Report no. 58. 16—17 September 1944. CARL.

U.S. Army Ground Forces. Immediate Report no. 63. HQ, 12th Army Group. 24 September 1944. Comments of Col. L. E. Jacoby CARL.

U.S. Army Ground Forces. Immediate Report no. 88. European Theater of Operations. 12th Army Group. 30 October 1944. CARL.

U.S. Army Ground Forces. Report no. 20 309. 25 November 1944. CARL.

U.S. Army Ground Forces. Board Report no. C-190. European Theater of Operations. 25 August 1944. CARL.

U.S. Army Ground Forces Board. Mediterranean Theater of Operations. "Tank Destroyer Conference, Florence, Italy." November 1944. CARL.

U.S. Army Ground Forces Board. Mediterranean Theater of Operations. "The Tank Destroyer Battalion in Action." Report A-Misc-21. 24 May 1944. CARL.

U.S. Army Ground Forces Board. North African Theater of Operations. Report A-165. 20 June 1944. CARL.

U.S. Army. 814th Tank Destroyer Battalion. After-Action Report. December 1944. CARL.

U.S. Army Tank Destroyer Center. "Tank Destroyer History." Camp Hood, TX, 1945? Microfilm, Library of Congress.

U.S. Forces, European Theater. General Board. "Report on Study of Organization, Equipment, and Tactical Employment of Tank Destroyer Units." [1946]. CARL.

Ward, Orlando. Papers. U.S. Army Military History Institute, Carlisle Barracks, PA.

Published

Great Britain. War Office. Notes from Theatres of War. No. 20. Italy 1943/1944. N.p., 1945.

U.S. Army Command and General Staff School. *Antimechanized Defense (Tentative)*. Fort Leavenworth, KS, 1939.

U.S. Army Command and General Staff School. *Antitank Defense (Tentative)*. Fort Leavenworth, KS, 1936.

U.S. Army Command and General Staff School. FM 101—10 (Tentative). *Staff Officer's Field Manual: Organization, Technical, and Logistical Data*. Fort Leavenworth, KS, [1943].

U.S. Army Infantry School. TC 7-24. *Antiarmor Techniques for Mechanized Infantry*. Fort Benning, GA, 1975.

U.S. Army Training and Doctrine Command. Regulation no. 11-7. *Operational Concepts and Army Doctrine*. Fort Monroe, VA, 1982.

U.S. War Department. FM 7—35. *Antitank Company, Infantry Regiment and Antitank Platoon, Infantry Battalion.* Washington, DC: U.S. Government Printing Office, 1944.

U.S. War Department. FM 18—5. *Tank Destroyer Field Manual, Organization and Tactics of Tank Destroyer Units.* Washington, DC: U.S. Government Printing Office, 1942.

U.S. War Department. FM 18—5. *Tactical Employment Tank Destroyer Unit.* Washington, DC: U.S. Government Printing Office, 1944.

U.S. War Department. FM 18—20. *Tactical Employment of Tank Destroyer Platoon Self-Propelled.* Washington, DC: U.S. Government Printing Office, 1944.

U.S. War Department. FM 100—5. *Tentative Field Service Regulations: Operations.* Washington, DC: U.S. Government Printing Office, 1939.

U.S. War Department. FM 100—5. *Field Service Regulations: Operations.* Washington, DC: U.S. Government Printing Office, 1941.

U.S. War Department. War Plans Division. "Instructions for Anti-tank Defense (Provisional—February 1918) from an Official British Document." War Department Document no. 783. April 1918.

Interviews and Letters

Clarke, Bruce C., interview with Gregory Fontenot. McLean, VA, 19 August 1984.

Green, Robert W. Letter to the author, 22 May 1977.

Hasbrouck, Robert W., interview with Gregory Fontenot. Washington, DC, 20 August 1984.

Books and Articles

"Artillery and the Tank." *Field Artillery Journal* 30 (July—August 1940): 243—48.

Baily, Charles M. *Faint Praise: American Tanks and Tank Destroyers During World War II.* Hamden, CT: Archon, 1983.

Bell, Paul B. "Tank Destroyers in the Roer River Crossing." *Field Artillery Journal* 35 (August 1945):497—98.

Betson, William R. "Sidi-Bou-Zid—A Case History of Failure." *Armor* 91 (November—December 1982):38—44.

Blumenson, Martin. *Breakout and Pursuit.* U.S. Army in World War II: The European Theater of Operations. 1961. Reprint. Washington, DC: Office of the Chief of Military History, U.S. Army, 1970.

Chamberlain, Peter, and Chris Ellis. *British and American Tanks of World War II.* New York: Arco, 1981.

Cole, Hugh M. *The Ardennes; Battle of the Bulge.* U.S. Army in World War II: The European Theater of Operations. 1965. Reprint. Washington, DC: Office of the Chief of Military History, U.S. Army, 1983.

Cole, Hugh M. *The Lorraine Campaign.* U.S. Army in World War II: The European Theater of Operations. 1950. Reprint. Washington, DC: Historical Division, U.S. Army, 1981.

Cooper, Matthew. *The German Army, 1933—1945.* New York: Bonanza, 1984.

Court, G. D. W. *Hard Pounding.* Washington, DC: The U.S. Field Artillery Association, 1946.

Cushman, Allerton. "Tank Destroyers Against Japan." *Field Artillery Journal* 36 (February 1946):70—73.

D'Este, Carlo. *Decision in Normandy.* New York: E. P. Dutton, 1983.

Doughty, Robert A. "French Antitank Doctrine 1940: The Antidote that Failed." *Military Review* 56 (May 1976):36—48.

Doughty, Robert A. *The Evolution of U.S. Army Doctrine, 1946—76.* Leavenworth Paper no. 1. Fort Leavenworth, KS: Combat Studies Institute, U.S. Army Command and General Staff College, 1979.

Dupont, Jean. "Fighting the Panzers." *Field Artillery Journal* 31 (August 1941):538—43.

Ellman, Gilbert A. "Panther vs. Panzer." *Military Review* 24 (August 1944): 21—26.

Gabel, Christopher R. "The U.S. Army GHQ Maneuvers of 1941." Ph.D. dissertation, Ohio State University, 1981. Microfilm. Ann Arbor, MI: University Microfilms International, 1981.

Greenfield, Kent Roberts, Robert R. Palmer, and Bell I. Wiley. *The Organization of Ground Combat Troops.* U.S. Army in World War II: The Army Ground Forces. Washington, DC: Historical Division, United States Army, 1947.

Hamilton, Nigel. *Master of the Battlefield: Monty's War Years, 1942—44.* New York: McGraw-Hill, 1983.

Horne, Alistair. *To Lose a Battle, France 1940.* Boston: Little, Brown and Co., 1969.

Howe, George F. *Northwest Africa: Seizing the Initiative in the West.* U.S. Army in World War II: The Mediterranean Theater of Operations. Washington, DC: Office of the Chief of Military History, Department of the Army, 1957.

Hunnicutt, R. P. *Sherman: A History of the American Medium Tank.* Novato, CA: Presidio Press, 1978.

Lemp, John, and Ernest C. Hatfield. "Tank Destroyers as Assault Guns." *Field Artillery Journal* 35 (April 1945):244—45.

Liddell Hart, Basil Henry. *The German Generals Talk.* New York: W. Morrow, 1948.

Macksey, Kenneth. *Tank Pioneers.* New York: Jane's Publishing, 1981.

McNelly, R. L. "Tank Destroyers at Work—Without the Book." *Field Artillery Journal* 35 (July 1945):396—98.

Marston, O. F. "Fast Moving Targets." *Field Artillery Journal* 30 (July—August 1940):264—67.

Meachem, P. C. "A New Fighting Team." *Field Artillery Journal* 34 (November 1944):778—80.

"New Tank Destroyer Battalions." *Infantry Journal* 50 (January 1942): 56—59.

"Newly Approved Organization, Division Artillery—Triangular Division." *Field Artillery Journal* 30 (September—October 1940):36—37.

Oborn, Eugene T. "Proper Use and Abuse of Tank Destroyers." *Field Artillery Journal* 35 (July 1945):398—99.

Ogorkiewicz, Richard M. *Armored Forces*. New York: Arco, 1970.

Sawicki, James A. *Tank Battalions of the U.S. Army*. Dumfries, VA: Wyvern, 1983.

"Second Battle of the Carolinas." *Time,* 8 December 1941:66.

Simpkin, Richard E. *Antitank; An Airmechanized Response to Armored Threats in the 90's*. New York: Brassey's, 1982.

Stanton, Shelby L. *Order of Battle: U.S. Army, World War II*. Novato, CA: Presidio Press, 1984.

Stubbs, Mary, and Stanley R. Connor. *Armor-Cavalry*. Pt. 1. *Regular Army and Army Reserve*. Army Lineage Series. Washington, DC: Office of the Chief of Military History, U.S. Army, 1969.

Thomson, Harry C., and Lida Mayo. *The Ordnance Department: Procurement and Supply*. U.S. Army in World War II: The Technical Services. Washington, DC: Office of the Chief of Military History, Department of the Army, 1960.

Van Wyck, Ralph. "Antitank Battery Training." *Field Artillery Journal* 30 (January 1941):6—10.

Wedemeyer, A. C. "Antitank Defense." *Field Artillery Journal* 31 (May 1941):258—72. Also, "Stopping the Armored Onslaught." *Infantry Journal* 48 (May 1941):22—31.

Weeks, John. *Men Against Tanks, A History of Antitank Warfare*. New York: Mason/Charter, 1975.

LEAVENWORTH PAPERS

1. *The Evolution of U.S. Army Tactical Doctrine, 1946—76*, by Major Robert A. Doughty

2. *Nomonhan: Japanese-Soviet Tactical Combat, 1939*, by Dr. Edward J. Drea

3. *"Not War But Like War": The American Intervention in Lebanon*, by Dr. Roger J. Spiller

4. *The Dynamics of Doctrine: The Changes in German Tactical Doctrine During the First World War*, by Captain Timothy T. Lupfer

5. *Fighting the Russians in Winter: Three Case Studies*, by Dr. Allen F. Chew

6. *Soviet Night Operations*, by Major Claude R. Sasso

7. *August Storm: The Soviet 1945 Strategic Offensive in Manchuria*, by Lieutenant Colonel David M. Glantz

8. *August Storm: Soviet Tactical and Operational Combat in Manchuria, 1945*, by Lieutenant Colonel David M. Glantz

9. *Defending the Driniumor: Covering Force Operations in New Guinea, 1944*, by Dr. Edward J. Drea

10. *Chemical Warfare in World War I: The American Experience, 1917—1918*, by Major(P) Charles E. Heller, USAR

11. *Rangers: Selected Combat Operations in World War II*, by Dr. Michael J. King

12. *Seek, Strike, and Destroy: U.S. Army Tank Destroyer Doctrine in World War II*, by Dr. Christopher R. Gabel

---

RESEARCH SURVEYS

1. *Amicicide: The Problem of Friendly Fire in Modern War*, by Lieutenant Colonel Charles R. Shrader

2. *Toward Combined Arms Warfare: A Survey of 20th-Century Tactics, Doctrine and Organization*, by Captain Jonathan M. House

3. *Rapid Deployment Logistics: Lebanon, 1958*, by Lieutenant Colonel Gary H. Wade

4. *The Soviet Airborne Experience*, by Lieutenant Colonel David M. Glantz

---

STUDIES IN PROGRESS

Counterattack on the Naktong: Light Infantry Operations in Korea, 1950

●

Standing Fast: German Defensive Doctrine
on the Russian Front During World War II

●

Tactics and Doctrine in Imperial Russia

●

U.S. Intervention in the Dominican Republic, 1965

●

Evolution of the Corps

●

World War II Eastern Front Atlas

●

Peacekeeping Operations

●

Mobilization Related Correlates of Success
in American World War II Infantry Divisions

●

Dragon Rouge: Hostage Rescue in the Congo

●

Light Infantry in Modern Historical Perspective

●

Abu-Ageila and Um Katef: History and Battle Planning

●

Counterguerrilla Operations: Nicaragua, 1927—33

●

World War II Corps Commander's Profile

☆ U.S. GOVERNMENT PRINTING OFFICE : 1986—652-003/22152